Edited by Herausgegeben von
Peter Körner, Maximilian Liesner, Peter Cachola Schmal

Contents Inhalt

4 **Foreword** Vorwort

Prize Winner, International Highrise Award 2018
Preisträger des Internationalen Hochhaus Preises 2018

9 General Jury Statement IHA 2018
Allgemeines Jurystatement zum IHP 2018

14 L. Benjamín Romano, Mexico City Mexiko-Stadt, **Mexico** Mexiko
TORRE REFORMA, Mexico City Mexiko-Stadt, **Mexico** Mexiko

20 Benjamín Romano in Conversation with im Gespräch mit Peter Cachola Schmal, Director Direktor Deutsches Architekturmuseum, Frankfurt am Main

34 Visit to the Prize Winner in Mexico City, June 2018 Reise zum Preisträger in Mexiko-Stadt, Juni 2018

38 Take into Account the Dark to Tell the Light Das Dunkle mitdenken, um das Helle zu erzählen
Alexander Gutzmer, Chief editor *Baumeister* magazine Chefredakteur *Baumeister*, **Munich** München

48 Locations of Projects Nominated Standorte der nominierten Projekte

Finalists, International Highrise Award 2018
Finalisten des Internationalen Hochhaus Preises 2018

50 Büro Ole Scheeren, Bangkok, Thailand;
OMA Office for Metropolitan Architecture, Beijing Peking, China
MAHANAKHON, Bangkok, Thailand

56 Herzog & de Meuron, Basel, Switzerland Schweiz
BEIRUT TERRACES, Beirut, Lebanon Libanon

62 MAD Architects, Beijing Peking, China
CHAOYANG PARK PLAZA, Beijing Peking, China

68 WOHA, Singapore Singapur
OASIA HOTEL DOWNTOWN, Singapore Singapur

Projects Nominated, International Highrise Award 2018
Nominierte Projekte des Internationalen Hochhaus Preises 2018

74 AL_A, London, UK Großbritannien
CENTRAL EMBASSY, Bangkok, Thailand

76 Ateliers Jean Nouvel, Paris, France Frankreich
LE NOUVEL KLCC, Kuala Lumpur, Malaysia

78 Büro Ole Scheeren, Hong Kong Hongkong, China
DUO, Singapore Singapur

80 David Chipperfield Architects, Berlin, Germany Deutschland
AMOREPACIFIC HEADQUARTERS, Seoul, South Korea Südkorea

82 Foster + Partners, London, UK Großbritannien;
Heatherwick Studio, London, UK Großbritannien
The Bund Finance Center, Shanghai, China

84 Francis-Jones Morehen Thorp, Sydney, Australia Australien
EY CENTRE, Sydney, Australia Australien

86 gmp Architekten von Gerkan, Marg und Partner, Hamburg, Germany Deutschland
GREENLAND CENTRAL PLAZA, Zhengzhou, China

88 gmp Architekten von Gerkan, Marg und Partner, Hamburg, Germany Deutschland
NANJING FINANCIAL CITY, Nanjing, China

90 Goettsch Partners, Chicago IL, USA
150 NORTH RIVERSIDE, Chicago IL, USA

92 Harry Gugger Studio, Basel, Switzerland Schweiz
THE EXCHANGE, Vancouver, Canada Kanada

94 Heller Manus Architects, San Francisco CA, USA
181 FREMONT, San Francisco CA, USA

The International Highrise Award Internationaler Hochhaus Preis 2018

96	Herzog & de Meuron, Basel, Switzerland Schweiz
56 LEONARD STREET, New York NY, USA
98	ingenhoven architects, Dusseldorf Düsseldorf, Germany Deutschland
MARINA ONE, Singapore Singapur
100	JAHN, Chicago IL, USA
50 WEST, New York NY, USA
102	Kohn Pedersen Fox Associates, New York NY, USA
LOTTE WORLD TOWER, Seoul, South Korea Südkorea
104	Kohn Pedersen Fox Associates, New York NY, USA
PING AN FINANCE CENTRE, Shenzhen, China
106	Meixner Schlüter Wendt Architekten, Frankfurt am Main, Germany Deutschland
NEUER HENNINGER TURM, Frankfurt am Main, Germany Deutschland
108	NBBJ, Los Angeles CA, USA
TENCENT SEAFRONT HEADQUARTERS, Shenzhen, China
110	Pelli Clarke Pelli Architects, New Haven CT, USA
SALESFORCE TOWER, San Francisco CA, USA
112	Renzo Piano Building Workshop, Paris, France Frankreich
TRIBUNAL DE PARIS, Paris, France Frankreich
114	SCDA Architects, Singapore Singapur
ECHELON, Singapore Singapur
116	SHoP Architects, New York NY, USA
461 DEAN STREET, New York NY, USA
118	SHoP Architects, New York NY, USA
AMERICAN COPPER BUILDINGS, New York NY, USA
120	SimpsonHaugh, London, UK Großbritannien
DOLLAR BAY, London, UK Großbritannien
122	Skidmore, Owings & Merrill LLP, San Francisco CA, USA
POLY INTERNATIONAL PLAZA, Beijing Peking, China
124	Skidmore, Owings & Merrill LLP, London, UK Großbritannien;
Squire & Partners, London, UK Großbritannien
THE LEXICON, London, UK Großbritannien
126	UNStudio, Amsterdam, Netherlands Niederlande
RAFFLES CITY, Hangzhou, China
128	UNStudio, Amsterdam, Netherlands Niederlande
THE SCOTTS TOWER, Singapore Singapur
130	WOHA, Singapore Singapur
HUAKU SKY GARDEN, Taipei Taipeh, Taiwan
132	Zaha Hadid Architects, London, UK Großbritannien
GENERALI TOWER, Milan Mailand, Italy Italien
134	Zaha Hadid Architects, London, UK Großbritannien
NANJING INTERNATIONAL CULTURAL CENTRE, Nanjing, China
136	Winners of the International Highrise Award 2004–2016
Preisträger Internationaler Hochhaus Preis 2004–2016
138	List of Projects, International Highrise Award 2004–2018
Projektliste Internationaler Hochhaus Preis 2004–2018
142	Imprint: Project Coordination Impressum Projektkoordination
Imprint: Catalogue Impressum Katalog
Imprint: Exhibition Impressum Ausstellung
144	Picture Credits Abbildungsnachweise

The International Highrise Award Internationaler Hochhaus Preis **2018**

Foreword

Dr Ina Hartwig
Deputy Mayor in charge of Culture of the City of Frankfurt am Main

Dr Matthias Danne
Member of the Management Board, DekaBank

Peter Cachola Schmal
Director, Deutsches Architekturmuseum (DAM)

36 projects from 15 different countries were nominated for this year's International Highrise Award. Preliminary research by the Deutsches Architekturmuseum confirmed that, over the last two years, China once again outranked every country in the world in terms of the number of high-rise buildings constructed on its soil. Approximately one in every three buildings with a height of at least 100 metres is erected in the Middle Kingdom, even if international architecture firms are often responsible for the planning. This extraordinary level of construction activity is also evident for the first time in the list of nominees, which includes nine projects in China.

The first three recipients of the International Highrise Award were pure office towers (in 2004, De Hoftoren in The Hague by Kohn Pedersen Fox; in 2006, Torre Agbar in Barcelona by Ateliers Jean Nouvel; in 2008, Hearst Tower in New York by Foster + Partners). A residential high-rise was honoured for the first time in 2010, with the selection of WOHA's The Met in Bangkok. This was followed in 2012 by another pure office tower: 1 Bligh Street in Sydney by ingenhoven architects + Architectus. But residential projects soon captured the award again – in 2014, with Stefano Boeris's Bosco Verticale in Milan; and in 2016, with VIA 57 West in New York by BIG – Bjarke Ingels Group.

In contrast to this internationally enduring trend toward residential towers as well as ever-larger mixed-use projects in Asia, this year's prize-winner – Torre Reforma by L. Benjamín Romano – is once again a classic office building. Here, however, it is only the type of usage that is conventional. The

Vorwort

Dr. Ina Hartwig
Kulturdezernentin der Stadt Frankfurt am Main

Dr. Matthias Danne
Mitglied des Vorstands der DekaBank

Peter Cachola Schmal
Direktor des Deutschen Architekturmuseums

In diesem Jahr wurden 36 Projekte aus 15 Ländern für die Auszeichnung mit dem Internationalen Hochhaus Preis nominiert. Bei der Vorrecherche des Deutschen Architekturmuseums bestätigte sich, dass auch in den vergangenen zwei Jahren wieder nirgendwo auf der Welt so viele Hochhäuser gebaut wurden wie in China. Ungefähr jedes dritte Gebäude mit einer Höhe von mindestens 100 Metern entsteht im Reich der Mitte, auch wenn für die Planungen häufig internationale Büros verantwortlich zeichnen. Diese enorme Bautätigkeit wird in diesem Jahr auch erstmalig anhand der Liste der Nominierten deutlich, die neun Projekte in China beinhaltet.

Die ersten drei Preisträger des Internationalen Hochhaus Preises waren reine Bürotürme (2004 De Hoftoren in Den Haag von Kohn Pedersen Fox, 2006 Torre Agbar in Barcelona von Ateliers Jean Nouvel, 2008 Hearst Tower in New York von Foster + Partners). Im Jahr 2010 wurde mit The Met in Bangkok von WOHA zum ersten Mal ein Wohnhochhaus ausgezeichnet. Danach folgte 2012 mit 1 Bligh Street in Sydney von ingenhoven architects + Architectus nochmals ein reines Bürogebäude. Aber bereits 2014 und 2016 gewannen mit Stefano Boeris Bosco Verticale in Mailand sowie VIA 57 West in New York von BIG – Bjarke Ingels Group die nächsten Wohnprojekte.

Entgegen diesem weltweit andauernden Trend hin zum Wohnturm sowie zu immer größeren mischgenutzten Projekten in Asien ist der diesjährige Preisträger Torre Reforma von L. Benjamín Romano wieder ein klassisches Bürogebäude. Dabei ist allerdings nur die Art der Nutzung konventionell. Die in Mexiko-Stadt vorherrschende Erdbebenproblematik erfordert ein kluges Tragwerkskonzept, das dem 246 Meter hohen Büroturm sein signifikantes Erscheinungsbild verleiht – und

International Highrise Award 2018: Jury session at DekaBank, Frankfurt am Main
Jurysitzung des Internationalen Hochhaus Preises 2018 in der DekaBank, Frankfurt am Main

prevailing problem of earthquakes in Mexico City calls for an intelligent support structure concept, which lends the 246-metre-high office tower its striking appearance – and in so doing places Mexico's capital on the world map of ground-breaking high-rise architecture. A no less fascinating aspect of the project's story is the unusual path to its financing (for more on this, see Peter Cachola Schmal's interview with Benjamín Romano, pp. 20–33), which ensured its careful planning down to the smallest detail and could thereby also serve as a blueprint for successful projects beyond Mexico's borders.

In accordance with the award rules, this year's winner was once again selected from among five finalists. It is notable here that each of these projects embodies a specific signature, which it actively communicates to the world at large.

MahaNakhon, one of two nominated projects by Büro Ole Scheeren, made it to the final five. Ole Scheeren began work on Thailand's tallest building while still at OMA and completed it with his own Chinese firm, which also has a location in Bangkok. Its distinctive pixelated façade makes the tower a new landmark of the capital as well as a symbol of the city's upswing and accompanying globalisation.

With its sculptural project Beirut Terraces, the Basel-based firm of Herzog & de Meuron aestheticize the theme of living in Mediterranean climates like that of Lebanon's capital. The staggered white floor slabs blur the transition between interior and exterior, resulting in a unique cultivation of open-air living.

The only nominated project located in China that was also designed by a Chinese architectural office is the work of MAD Architects from Beijing. The Chaoyang Park Plaza complex, also in Beijing, was inspired by traditional landscape painting. Due to its dark glass façade and amorphous shapes, it stands out strikingly from the repetitive construction surrounding it. In this way, it exemplifies an interesting, identity-defining approach to the development of a contemporary, uniquely Chinese architectural language.

Mexikos Hauptstadt damit auf die Weltkarte wegweisender Hochhausarchitektur setzt. Ein nicht minder spannender Aspekt ist der ungewöhnliche Weg der Projektfinanzierung (siehe dazu Benjamín Romano im Interview mit Peter Cachola Schmal, S. 20–33), der Garant für eine sorgfältige Planung bis ins kleinste Detail war und deswegen auch über Mexiko hinaus als Blaupause für erfolgreiche Projekte dienen könnte.

Auch in diesem Jahr ging der Preisträger gemäß den Statuten aus fünf Finalisten hervor. Dabei fällt auf, dass alle Projekte eine spezifische Handschrift haben und diese offensiv nach außen kommunizieren.

Als eines von zwei nominierten Projekten des Büro Ole Scheeren hat es MahaNakhon unter die Finalisten geschafft. Ole Scheeren begann die Arbeit am höchsten Gebäude Thailands noch bei OMA, vollendete sie dann aber in seinem eigenen chinesischen Büro mit einer Niederlassung auch in Bangkok. Der Turm mit seiner charakteristischen Pixelfassade ist ein neues Wahrzeichen der Hauptstadt und zugleich Sinnbild für den Aufschwung der Metropole und die damit einhergehende Globalisierung.

Mit ihrem skulpturalen Projekt Beirut Terraces ästhetisieren Herzog & de Meuron aus Basel das Thema Wohnen in mediterranem Klima wie in Libanons Hauptstadt. Die weißen und gegeneinander verschobenen Geschossplatten verwischen den Übergang zwischen Innen und Außen. So wird das Leben im Freien auf einzigartige Weise kultiviert.

Das unter den Nominierten einzige Projekt in China, das auch von einem chinesischen Büro entworfen wurde, stammt von MAD Architects aus Peking. Der Komplex Chaoyang Park Plaza, ebenfalls in Peking, ist von traditioneller Landschaftsmalerei inspiriert und hebt sich durch seine dunklen Glasfassaden sowie die amorphen Formen deutlich von der umliegenden repetitiven Bebauung ab. Er verkörpert somit einen interessanten, identitätsstiftenden Ansatz zur Entwicklung einer eigenen chinesischen Architektursprache der Gegenwart.

WOHA setzen ihren Weg des begrünten Hochhauses mit dem Oasia Hotel Downtown konsequent fort und reduzieren es auf ein bepflanztes Exoskelett, das beeindruckende Freiräume umschließt. Geschützt vor

WOHA continue to pursue their goal of green highrise buildings with the Oasia Hotel Downtown, reducing the structure to an exoskeleton with impressive open spaces. These are protected from sun and rain and thus create natural oases with excellent residential quality in the midst of Singapore's extremely dense city centre – an exemplary model for other tropical metropolises and megacities.

The International Highrise Award was established in 2003 by the City of Frankfurt am Main, in particular the Deutsches Architekturmuseum, and DekaBank; it was presented for the first time in 2004. Since then, it has been organised and financed cooperatively on a biannual basis. This year, the award ceremony in the Frankfurt Paulskirche will thus be taking place for the eighth time.

Frankfurt has a long tradition of skyscraper construction. Its skyline, which has grown ever since the end of the Second World War, was not only unique in Germany for several decades, it was also trailblazing for Europe as a whole. Limited building space and the growing demand for office accommodation necessitated a very dense city centre, which could only be achieved with this type of construction. Frankfurt's skyscrapers shape today's city skyline and epitomise the success and self-confidence of this compact metropolis. Currently, several new towers are under construction or in the planning stages.

With its continuing commitment to the International Highrise Award, the City of Frankfurt demonstrates its consistent position, according to which the crucial factor in high-rise construction is not only altitude, but also a convincing overall approach with regard to efficiency, integration in the urban context, design and technology as well as the quality of life. For this reason, the International Highrise Award focuses on structures with a minimum height of 100 metres which represent outstanding contributions to the evolution of high-rise architecture around the world.

For DekaBank, the presentation of the International Highrise Award has been an important part of its social commitment since the joint establishment of the award 15 years ago. In that time the award has gained international recognition, thanks to the continuing development of the project and the close cooperation of the three founding partners. DekaBank is the investment division of the Sparkasse financial group. With its subsidiaries, DekaBank forms the Deka Group. Its Real Estate Segment pools the Deka Group's worldwide property expertise. Through its commitment to the International Highrise Award, Deka aims to draw attention to innovative, future-oriented, yet efficient construction.

The Deutsches Architekturmuseum (DAM) observes the continuing worldwide boom of this showpiece discipline in twenty-first-century architecture. The biannual granting of the award ensures significant documentation as well as a long-term analysis of contemporary high-rise development. The current building activity in China is a subject of particular

Sonne und Regen schaffen die Architekten naturnahe Oasen mit enormer Aufenthaltsqualität inmitten des stark verdichteten Stadtzentrums von Singapur – beispielhaft für Metropolen und Megacitys in den Tropen.

Der Internationale Hochhaus Preis wurde 2003 gemeinsam von der Stadt Frankfurt am Main, insbesondere dem Deutschen Architekturmuseum, und der DekaBank initiiert und 2004 zum ersten Mal vergeben. Seitdem wird er alle zwei Jahre kooperativ organisiert und finanziert. Somit findet in diesem Jahr die Preisverleihung in der Frankfurter Paulskirche zum achten Mal statt.

In Frankfurt am Main hat der Hochhausbau Tradition. Die seit dem Zweiten Weltkrieg wachsende Skyline war über Jahrzehnte nicht nur singulär in Deutschland, sondern auch richtungsweisend für Europa. Aufgrund der begrenzten Bauflächen und der wachsenden Nachfrage nach Büroräumen wurde eine innerstädtische Dichte erforderlich, die nur mit diesem Gebäudetyp erreicht werden konnte. Die Hochhäuser prägen heute das Stadtbild und symbolisieren den Erfolg und das Selbstbewusstsein der kleinen Metropole. Aktuell befinden sich gleich mehrere Türme im Bau und in der Planung.

Mit ihrem andauernden Engagement für den Internationalen Hochhaus Preis verdeutlicht die Stadt Frankfurt am Main ihre konsequente Haltung, wonach im Hochhausbau nicht allein die Höhenmeter, sondern vielmehr überzeugende Gesamtkonzepte in Bezug auf Wirtschaftlichkeit, Einbindung in den urbanen Kontext, Design und Technik sowie Aufenthaltsqualität maßgebend sind. Ein besonderes Augenmerk liegt dabei auf ökologischen Aspekten. Somit richtet sich der Internationale Hochhaus Preis an Bauten mit einer Mindesthöhe von 100 Metern, die herausragende Beiträge zur Evolution der Hochhausarchitektur weltweit darstellen.

Für die DekaBank ist die Verleihung des Internationalen Hochhaus Preises seit der gemeinsamen Gründung vor 15 Jahren ein wichtiger Teil ihres gesellschaftlichen Engagements. Durch die kontinuierliche Weiterentwicklung des Preises und die dabei gewachsene, vertrauensvolle Zusammenarbeit der drei Partner hat sich die Auszeichnung internationale Anerkennung erworben. Die DekaBank, das Wertpapierhaus der Sparkassen, bildet gemeinsam mit ihren Tochtergesellschaften die Deka-Gruppe. Das Geschäftsfeld Immobilien bündelt die weltweite Immobilienkompetenz der Deka-Gruppe. Mit ihrem Engagement für den Internationalen Hochhaus Preis möchte die Deka den Fokus auf innovatives, zukunftsweisendes und trotzdem wirtschaftliches Bauen richten.

Das Deutsche Architekturmuseum (DAM) begleitet den weltweit andauernden Boom der architektonischen Paradedisziplin des 21. Jahrhunderts. Anhand der zweijährlichen Vergabe des Preises entstehen eine aussagekräftige Dokumentation sowie eine Langzeitanalyse der zeitgenössischen Hochhausentwicklung. Besonders interessant zu beobachten ist momentan sicherlich das Baugeschehen in China. Ungeachtet dessen, dass sich nur ein chinesisches Projekt unter den Finalisten befindet, ist eine deutliche Qualitätssteigerung erkennbar, die dort zukünftige Preisträger vermuten lässt. Aktuell sind aber nach wie vor New York und Singapur die spannendsten Zentren des Hochhausbaus.

On the left Links: **Thomas Demand**, Prize Winner's sculpture for the International Highrise Award Statuette für den Internationalen Hochhaus Preis, **Titanium and Granite** Titan und Granit, 36 x 15 x 12 cm

Jurors of the International Highrise Award 2018 Juroren des Internationalen Hochhaus Preises 2018 **From left to right** Von links nach rechts: **Sean Anderson** (Associate Curator for Architecture and Design Kurator für Architektur und Design, **Museum of Modern Art MoMA, New York City**); **Knut Stockhusen** (Structural engineer Tragwerksplaner / **Partner, schlaich bergermann partner, Stuttgart**); **Horst R. Muth** (Head of Real Estate Management Leiter Projektmanagement Immobilien, **Deka Immobilien GmbH, Frankfurt am Main**); **Peter Cachola Schmal** (Director Direktor **Deutsches Architekturmuseum DAM, Frankfurt am Main**); **Jette Cathrin Hopp** (Project Director Projektleiterin / Senior Architect Leitende Architektin, **Snøhetta, Oslo**); **Kai-Uwe Bergmann** (Architect Architekt / Partner, **BIG – Bjarke Ingels Group, New York City / Copenhagen** Kopenhagen); **Dr. Ina Hartwig** (Deputy Mayor in charge of Culture Kulturdezernentin, **Frankfurt am Main**); **Prof. Ulrike Lauber** (Architect Architektin / Principal Geschäftsführerin, **lauber zottmann blank architekten, Munich** München); **Thomas Schmengler** (Managing Director Geschäftsführer, **Deka Immobilien GmbH, Frankfurt am Main**)

interest. Notwithstanding the fact that only one Chinese project ranks among this year's finalists, one can observe a significant improvement in quality, which leads to speculations about future award winners from this nation. At the moment, however, New York and Singapore remain the most exciting centres for skyscraper construction.

The trend toward residential high-rises continues, as confirmed by the projects nominated for the International Highrise Award 2018. Now that this development, which originated in Asia, has belatedly arrived in Europe, an increasing number of residential towers are also being constructed in the West. Meanwhile, in Asia, the concept of the mixed-use building is already becoming established – combining work and residential spaces (and sometimes much more) under a single roof. Generally, the necessity of building upwards goes without saying: due to continuous migration into the major cities and ever-increasing populations, the high-rise is sure to represent the characteristic architectural typology of the coming decades.

Der Trend zum Wohnhochhaus hält an, wie die für den Internationalen Hochhaus Preis 2018 nominierten Projekte untermauern. Nachdem dieser Typus aus Asien mit Verspätung in Europa eingetroffen war, werden mittlerweile auch in der westlichen Welt vermehrt Wohntürme errichtet – während sich im asiatischen Raum unterdessen bereits das Konzept der mischgenutzten Gebäude verfestigt, die Arbeiten, Wohnen und zum Teil noch viel mehr unter einem Dach vereinen. Dass überhaupt in die Höhe gebaut werden muss, steht dabei außer Frage. Denn durch den kontinuierlichen Zuzug in die Metropolen und die weiter steigenden Bevölkerungszahlen wird das Hochhaus die maßgeblich prägende Bautypologie der kommenden Jahrzehnte darstellen.

General Jury Statement IHA 2018

"What does the building give back?" This was the fundamental question jury chair Kai-Uwe Bergmann of BIG – Bjarke Ingels Group (winner of the IHA 2016) posed as the main criterion for evaluating the "overall excellence" of the projects nominated in the competition for the International Highrise Award 2018. And there were quite a number, 36 in all: a challenging task for the jury.

The range of nominees this year was also particularly diverse, with the Asian candidates predominating, led by China and Singapore. While the USA followed this lead, Europe was this time hardly represented. Noticeably, European Architects are currently not designing buildings for their home continent.

The winner of the International Highrise Award 2018, by unanimous decision, is Torre Reforma by L. Benjamín Romano. The concrete-and-steel office building in Mexico City is 246 metres high and was completed in late 2016. Conceived as a huge urban obelisk and defined by two exposed-concrete walls arranged as an open book, Torre Reforma boasts architectural spaces designed to serve as a vertical continuation of the city.

Summing up the discussion, Kai-Uwe Bergmann enthused: "Torre Reforma is one of the most complex high-rise projects I've ever seen. Benjamín Romano has been extremely bold, taken his chances and in the process come up with a highly intelligent approach. He has created a distinctly local typology for a location on the main avenue in Mexico City. The solution he has found not only looks but is completely unconventional. It is a high-rise with two thoroughly different views, so that driving toward it you could be mistaken for not recognizing it if you only knew it from the one side." Further, Ina Hartwig, Deputy Mayor of the City of Frankfurt in charge of Culture, alluded to the vistas from the other side, namely from the tower which "offers great views over one of the largest downtown parks world-wide."

Jury member Jette Cathrin Hopp of Snøhetta added that "Romano has truly combined well-known technology in a compellingly innovative manner." Ulrike Lauber, principal of the architectural practice lauber zottmann blank, praised the perfect blend of aesthetics and engineering, resulting in "a support-free interior structure and complex earthquake-proofing." Knut Stockhusen, structural engineer and partner at schlaich bergermann partner, continued that "Romano has taken basic steel structures, nothing fancy, as his exo-skeleton, but he has then deployed them in a way that fits perfectly with the overall concrete façade. The perforation of the concrete walls takes the rigidity out of the façade, which would otherwise have been a risk to its survival during one of the city's numerous earthquakes. Romano thus creates a high-rise that is as beautiful as it is resilient."

Sean Anderson, Associate Curator for Architecture and Design at the MoMA, stated that Torre Reforma

While the two sides of Torre Reforma that face the downtown resemble a gigantic concrete sculpture ...
Während der Torre Reforma an den beiden Seiten Richtung Innenstadt die Form einer gigantischen Betonskulptur einnimmt, ...

Allgemeines Jurystatement zum IHP 2018

„Was gibt das Gebäude zurück?" Das war die grundlegende Frage, die der Juryvorsitzende Kai-Uwe Bergmann von BIG – Bjarke Ingels Group (Gewinner des IHP 2016) zum wichtigsten Bewertungskriterium für die „umfassende Qualität" der Projekte erklärte, die für den Internationalen Hochhaus Preis 2018 nominiert waren. Und mit 36 Einreichungen gab es von ihnen recht viele, was die Jury vor eine große Herausforderung stellte.

Auch die Bandbreite der Nominierten war in diesem Jahr besonders groß, wobei die asiatischen Kandidaten, angeführt von China und Singapur, dominierten. Es folgten die USA, während Europa dieses Mal abfiel. Dabei wurde deutlich, dass die europäischen Architekten ihre Bauten momentan nicht für den heimischen Kontinent entwerfen.

Der Gewinner des Internationalen Hochhaus Preises 2018 ist nach einstimmiger Entscheidung der Torre Reforma von L. Benjamín Romano. Der Büroturm aus Beton und Stahl in Mexiko-Stadt ist 246 Meter hoch und wurde Ende 2016 fertiggestellt. Wie ein riesiger urbaner Obelisk oder ein geöffnetes Buch zwischen zwei Sichtbetonwänden trumpft der Torre Reforma mit architektonischen Räumen auf, die als vertikale Fortsetzung der Stadt fungieren.

Begeistert fasste Kai-Uwe Bergmann die Diskussion zusammen: „Der Torre Reforma ist eines der komplexesten Hochhausprojekte, die ich je gesehen habe. Benjamín Romano war hier extrem wagemutig, ist viele Risiken eingegangen und hat dadurch einen hochintelligenten Ansatz gefunden. Seine Lösung sieht nicht nur völlig unkonventionell aus, sondern ist es auch. Ihm ist eine unmissverständlich lokale Typologie für einen Standort auf der Prachtstraße von Mexiko-Stadt gelungen. Das Hochhaus bietet zwei völlig unterschiedliche Ansichten, sodass man es beinahe nicht wiedererkennen würde, würde man es nur von einer Seite kennen." Ina Hartwig, die Kulturdezernentin der Stadt Frankfurt am Main, äußerte sich begeistert von der Aussicht in anderer Richtung, nämlich vom Turm aus, der „einen großartigen Blick über einen der größten Innenstadtparks der Welt bietet".

Jurymitglied Jette Cathrin Hopp von Snøhetta fügte hinzu: „Romano hat vertraute Technologien auf bestechend innovative Weise miteinander kombiniert." Ulrike Lauber, Mitinhaberin des Architekturbüros lauber zottmann blank, lobte die perfekte Verschmelzung von Ästhetik und Ingenieurskunst, die „stützenfreie Innenräume und eine komplexe Erdbebensicherheit" hervorbringt. Knut Stockhusen, Tragwerksplaner und Partner bei schlaich bergermann partner, führte fort: „Romano hat einfache Stahlkonstruktionen als Exoskelett gewählt, nichts Ausgefallenes, aber dann hat er sie auf eine Art und Weise eingesetzt, die perfekt zur Betonfassade passt. Die Perforation der Betonwände lockert die Starrheit der Fassade auf, die ansonsten bei den zahlreichen Erdbeben in der Stadt zu einem Risikofaktor geworden wäre. So schafft Romano ein Hochhaus, das sowohl schön als auch widerstandsfähig ist."

Sean Anderson, Kurator für Architektur und Design am MoMA, sah im Torre Reforma „das perfekte Zeugnis

"is perfect testimony to the fact that architecture in Mexico today is so innovative and engaging. Small wonder that it is not just LEED Platinum certified, but ably incorporates the city's history into its own fabric." In this regard, DekaBank's real estate experts Thomas Schmengler and Horst R. Muth singled out for particular admiration "the persuasively cautious treatment of the substance of the heritage-listed villa, which was first temporarily removed in its entirety and then restored to its original location while being integrated into the new build."

Finally, the director of Deutsches Architekturmuseum (DAM), Peter Cachola Schmal, was impressed by the architect's business model: "Benjamín Romano shows us that a single architect can redefine the standards of building and construction in his field and in his city. First he won investors over, bought the plot, developed the scheme, invented a massive structure that defied common skin-and-bone concepts and got his structural designers to follow this lead. And then he built it and rented it out. We are astonished that such a holistic approach is possible today and are stunned by the awesome result. He proved to us that this approach can really be a game-changer in certain countries."

On the way to their decision, the jury's wide-ranging discussion considered how a high-rise contributes to the urban fabric and how it encourages street life. The following aspects were analyzed, among others: the overall narrative, the sculptural qualities, the structural concept, the mix of uses, and the balance between commerce and culture. The resulting shortlist consisted of five finalists: Torre Reforma (Mexico City; L. Benjamín Romano), Beirut Terraces (Beirut; Herzog & de Meuron), Oasia Hotel Downtown (Singapore; WOHA), Chaoyang Park Plaza (Beijing; MAD Architects), and MahaNakhon (Bangkok; Büro Ole Scheeren).

Surprisingly, not a single European or US building made the final round, and only one of the honoured architectural practices is based in Europe. Of the one Mexican, one Middle Eastern and three Asian projects concerned, each finds a unique interpretation of its typology, be it for a resilient office tower (Torre Reforma), a stacked residential highrise (Beirut Terraces), a mixed-use high-rise garden (Oasia Hotel Downtown), an ensemble in a new indigenous vernacular (Chaoyang Park Plaza), or a hotel in the shape of a pixelated sculpture (MahaNakhon).

Torre Reforma was the one building that inspired both the structural engineers and the architects in like measure as a masterful demonstration of a new approach to the high-rise – and was therefore a worthy winner. It is a building that the entire jury felt did indeed embody the mission that Benjamín Romano set himself: "sustainable architecture, architectural structuring, high-tech and artistic integration".

dafür, wie innovativ und beeindruckend Architektur in Mexiko heute ist. Da verwundert es kaum, dass es nicht nur mit LEED-Platin zertifiziert wurde, sondern außerdem noch gekonnt einen Teil der Stadtgeschichte in seine Architektur integriert". Auch die Experten der Deka Immobilien GmbH, Thomas Schmengler und Horst R. Muth, betonten „den überzeugend behutsamen Umgang mit der Substanz der denkmalgeschützten Villa, die im Zuge der Bauarbeiten vorübergehend vollständig verschoben und anschließend, zurück am Originalstandort, in das neue Bauwerk integriert wurde".

Der Direktor des Deutschen Architekturmuseums (DAM), Peter Cachola Schmal, zeigte sich besonders vom Geschäftsmodell des Architekten beeindruckt: „Benjamín Romano beweist, dass ein einziger Architekt die Baustandards auf seinem Gebiet und in seiner Stadt neu definieren kann. Zuerst hat er Investoren gewonnen, das Grundstück erworben, den Entwurf entwickelt, eine massive Konstruktion fernab aller üblichen Haut-und-Knochen-Konzepte erdacht und seine Statiker davon überzeugt, seiner Idee zu folgen. Und dann hat er es gebaut und vermietet. Wir sind erstaunt, dass eine solch ganzheitliche Herangehensweise heutzutage möglich ist, und sind überwältigt von diesem fantastischen Resultat. Romano zeigt uns, dass dieser Ansatz in bestimmten Ländern wirklich etwas bewegen kann."

Auf dem Weg zur Entscheidung ging es in der breiten Diskussion der Jury unter anderem darum, wie ein Hochhaus zum Stadtgefüge und urbanen Leben beiträgt. Darüber hinaus wurden unter anderem folgende Aspekte analysiert: die übergreifende Aussage, die skulpturalen Qualitäten, das statische Konzept, die Nutzungsmischung sowie die Balance zwischen Wirtschaft und Kultur. Das Ergebnis war die Shortlist mit fünf Finalisten: Torre Reforma (Mexiko-Stadt; L. Benjamín Romano), Beirut Terraces (Beirut; Herzog & de Meuron), Oasia Hotel Downtown (Singapur; WOHA), Chaoyang Park Plaza (Peking; MAD Architects) und MahaNakhon (Bangkok; Büro Ole Scheeren).

Überraschenderweise schaffte es kein einziges europäisches oder US-amerikanisches Gebäude in die Finalrunde und nur eines der ausgezeichneten Architekturbüros hat seinen Sitz in Europa. Das mexikanische, das nahöstliche und die drei asiatischen Projekte finden eine je einzigartige Interpretation ihrer Topologie – sei es ein agiler Büroturm (Torre Reforma), ein gestapelter Wohnturm (Beirut Terraces), ein mischgenutzter Hochhausgarten (Oasia Hotel Downtown), ein lokal verwurzeltes Ensemble (Chaoyang Park Plaza) oder ein Hotel in Gestalt einer verpixelten Skulptur (MahaNakhon).

Der Torre Reforma war das Gebäude, das sowohl die Ingenieure als auch die Architekten in gleichem Maße begeisterte – als meisterhafter Ausdruck eines neuen Nachdenkens über das Hochhaus und somit als würdiger Preisträger. Es ist ein Gebäude, das in den Augen der gesamten Jury all das verkörpert, was sich Benjamín Romano selbst zum Ziel gesetzt hat: „nachhaltige Architektur, architektonische Gliederung, High-Tech und deren künstlerische Verbindung."

... with its third, fully glazed façade it opens up to the adjacent park.
... öffnet er sich mit seiner dritten, vollverglasten Seite zum angrenzenden Park.

pp. 12–13
Accessible to employees and guests, the terrace is the centrepiece of the tower.
S. 12–13
Die für alle Beschäftigten und Gäste zugängliche Terrasse ist das Herzstück in der Mitte des Gebäudes.

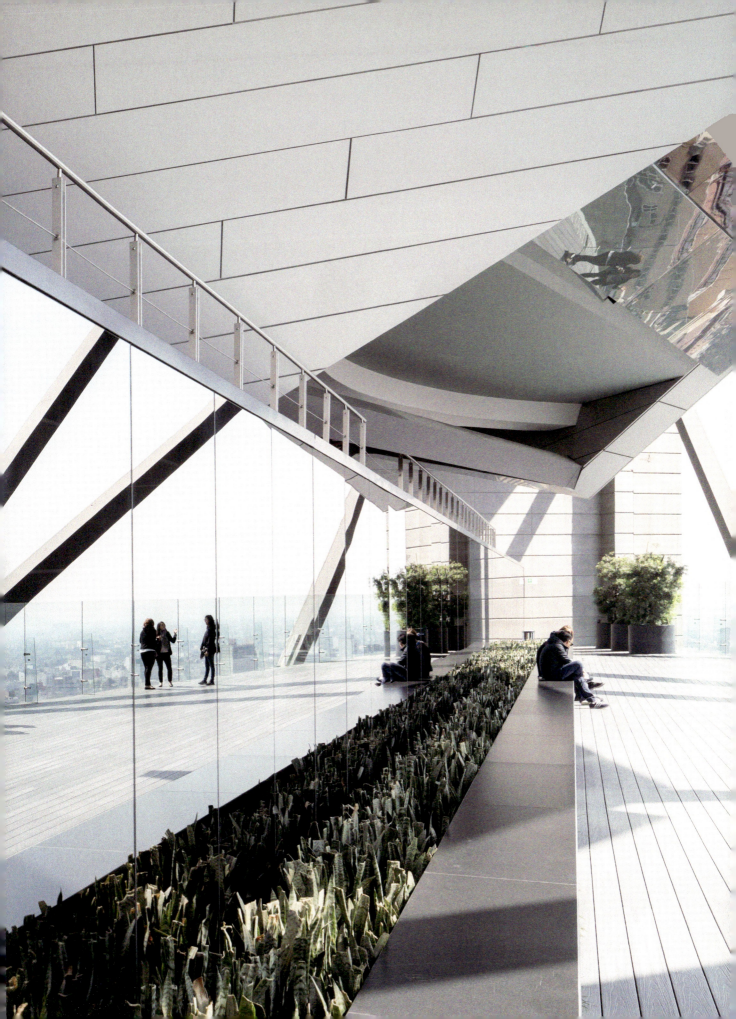

Prize Winner 2018
Preisträger 2018

L. Benjamín Romano
TORRE REFORMA
Mexico City Mexiko-Stadt, **Mexico** Mexiko

Architects Architekten **L. Benjamín Romano, Mexico City** Mexiko-Stadt, **Mexico** Mexiko
Project architect Projektarchitekt **L. Benjamín Romano**
Project team Projektteam
Octavio Aguilar, Lucía Alonso, Rafael Arce, Guillermo Arriola, César Balmes, Miriam Barajas, Julieta Boy, Jesús Hidalgo, Erick Islas, Harón Kababie, Ilan Kellersztain, Lilian Levy, Walter Lingard, Antonella Morittu, Mario Salim, Andrés Souto, Daniel Vega
Client Bauherr **Fondo Hexa, S.A. de C.V.**
Structural engineers Tragwerksplanung **Arup New York; Dr. Rodolfo Valles Mattox / DITEC**
MEP Haustechnik **Arup Los Angeles**

Height Höhe **246 m**
Storeys Geschosse **57**
Site area Grundstücksfläche **2788 m²**
Ground footprint Bebaute Fläche **2541 m²**
Gross floor area Bruttogeschossfläche **87 000 m²**
Structure Konstruktion **Composite** Verbundbauweise
Completion Fertigstellung **November 2016**
Main use Hauptnutzung **Office** Büros

Sustainability
Nachhaltigkeit
LEED Platinum Certification; committed to being carbon-neutral by 2030; rain and waste water are 100 % reused for the air-conditioning cooling towers with zero drainage to the city's sewage system; naturally ventilated patios; horizontal aluminium shades protect glass façade; robotic parking system places 480 cars free of toxic fumes; thanks to a floor height of three metres the garage can be transformed into office space should traffic be redirected; each cluster's MEP is monitored separately to optimize the energy efficiency; 80,000 trees newly planted citywide as stipulated by building permit
LEED-Platin-Zertifizierung; verpflichtet sich zur CO_2-Neutralität bis 2030; Regen- und Abwasser werden vollständig für die Kühltürme der Klimaanlage wiedergenutzt ohne Abfluss in die städtische Kanalisation; natürlich belüftete Patios; horizontale Sonnenblenden aus Aluminium verschatten die Glasfassade; automatisches System parkt 480 Autos ohne Abgasausstoß; Parkhaus kann wegen der Geschosshöhe von drei Metern nach einer möglichen Verkehrswende in Büroflächen umgewandelt werden; zur Optimierung der Energieeffizienz wird die Gebäudetechnik jedes Clusters einzeln überprüft; stadtweit 80 000 neu gepflanzte Bäume als Bestandteil der Baugenehmigung

Section
Schnitt

Functional diagrams:
Upper row: Structural system, Restaurants and sports, Patios and green areas, Offices, Core,
Lower row: Lifts, Electrical engineering, Hydraulic engineering, Wastewater treatment, Parking
Funktionsdiagramme:
Obere Reihe: Statisches Prinzip, Restaurants und Sport, Patios und Grünflächen, Büros, Kern
Untere Reihe: Aufzüge, Elektrotechnik, Wasserbau, Abwasseraufbereitung, Parkplätze

Barely perceptible from ground level but obvious from above, the tower expands noticeably as it rises.
Was vom Boden aus kaum wahrnehmbar ist, wird aus der Luft offensichtlich: Nach oben hin dehnt sich der Turm deutlich aus.

Technical know-how and artistic aspirations contributed in equal measure to the unique shape of Torre Reforma. This is especially apparent in the conception of the building's two massive outer walls, which are made of exposed concrete. They were poured little by little during the construction process: always one layer per day; always exactly 70 centimetres high. Because concrete takes on varying shades of grey during the pouring process depending upon the current humidity, Benjamín Romano decided to create a rhythmically hatched façade, thus avoiding the appearance of an irregular or even blotchy surface. The seams between the individual layers also serve as predetermined breaking points in the event of an earthquake, offering the forces at work a point of attack that does not affect the building's static equilibrium. Moreover, the building can move with the forces since large openings in the solid walls act as 'crumple zones', and the steel braces which carry the floors merge into flexible hinges in front of the glass façade. This concept has already proved highly successful. During the severe earthquake of September 2017, the only effect was a handful of fine, harmless cracks in the concrete seams.

Technisches Know-how und künstlerischer Anspruch haben gleichermaßen zur einzigartigen Form des Torre Reforma beigetragen. Besonders deutlich wird dies in der Konzeption der zwei massiven Außenwände aus Sichtbeton. Sie wurden im Bauprozess nach und nach gegossen: immer eine Schicht pro Tag und immer genau 70 Zentimeter hoch. Weil Beton während des Gießprozesses je nach herrschender Luftfeuchtigkeit unterschiedliche Grautöne annimmt, entschied sich Benjamín Romano für eine rhythmische Schraffur der Fassade. So konnte der Eindruck einer unregelmäßigen oder gar fleckigen Oberfläche vermieden werden. Die Fugen zwischen den einzelnen Schichten dienen dabei auch als Sollbruchstellen im Falle eines Erdbebens. Sie bieten den wirkenden Kräften einen Angriffspunkt, der die Statik nicht beeinträchtigt. Außerdem kann sich das Gebäude mitbewegen, weil große Öffnungen als „Knautschzonen" aus den massiven Wänden ausgespart sind und die Stahlstreben, die die Geschosse tragen, vor der Glasfassade in beweglichen Gelenken zusammenlaufen. Während des schweren Erdbebens im September 2017 hat sich dieses Konzept bereits als wirkungsvoll erwiesen. Zurück blieben nur ein paar feine, ungefährliche Risse in den Betonfugen.

The auditorium almost seems to float above the terrace.
Über der Terrasse scheint das Auditorium beinahe zu schweben.

The striking setback of the façade has its origins in a building regulation but adds to the iconic image of the tower.
Der markante Rücksprung der Fassade ist ursprünglich das Resultat einer Bauvorschrift, aber trägt zum ikonischen Erscheinungsbild des Turms bei.

The 70-centimetre-high concrete layers of the façade are carefully maintained, even at a dizzying height.
Auch in schwindelerregenden Höhen wird die Fassade aus je 70 Zentimeter hohen Betonschichten sorgsam instandgehalten.

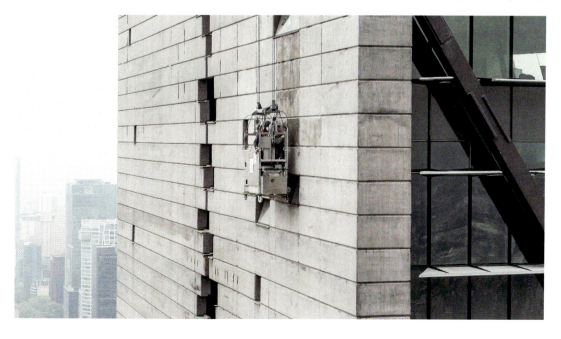

Beginning at a height of 200 metres, one of the two concrete walls bends strikingly inward. This feature is a response to Mexico City's building regulations: the skyscrapers on Paseo de la Reforma may be no more than twice as high as the width of the street. If a building exceeds this height, the upper part has to be recessed or tapered. Due to Romano's creative handling of this regulation, the building, depending on the viewer's perspective, changes not only its materiality but also its sculptural form.

With its characteristic triangular footprint, Torre Reforma reacts to the L-shape of the historic villa, so that its two concrete walls connect with the older structure to form a square at ground level. The resulting space defines the public foyer. The entire width of the building's third, glass side opens onto the Bosque de Chapultepec city park. In order to create additional usable space, the storeys here break free from the narrow corset of the triangle. To the front, the seemingly smooth façade forms a nearly imperceptible fourth corner. This angle projects further and further outward as the building's height increases, with the result that the most attractive, uppermost storeys, despite the sloping façade, boast the largest surface area.

Ab einer Höhe von 200 Metern knickt eine der beiden Betonwände auffällig nach innen ab. Grund dafür sind die Bauvorschriften von Mexiko-Stadt. Die Hochhäuser am Paseo de la Reforma dürfen maximal doppelt so hoch sein, wie die Straße breit ist. Soll ein Gebäude höher sein, ist ein Rücksprung oder eine Verjüngung vorgegeben. Durch Romanos kreativen Umgang mit dieser Vorschrift ändert sich je nach Blickwinkel nicht nur die Materialität des Gebäudes, sondern auch seine skulpturale Form.

Mit seiner charakteristischen dreieckigen Grundfläche reagiert der Torre Reforma auf die L-Form der historischen Villa, sodass sich die beiden Betonwände am Boden mit ihr zu einem Quadrat verbinden. Der so entstehende Raum definiert das öffentliche Foyer. Die dritte, verglaste Seite des Turms öffnet sich in ihrer gesamten Breite zum Stadtpark Bosque de Chapultepec. Um zusätzliche Nutzfläche zu schaffen, sprengen die Geschosse hier das enge Korsett des Dreiecks. Die scheinbar ebene Fassade bildet nach vorne eine beinahe nicht wahrnehmbare vierte Ecke. Diese kragt mit zunehmender Höhe immer weiter aus, wodurch die attraktivsten, obersten Geschosse trotz der abgeschrägten Fassade die größte Fläche aufweisen.

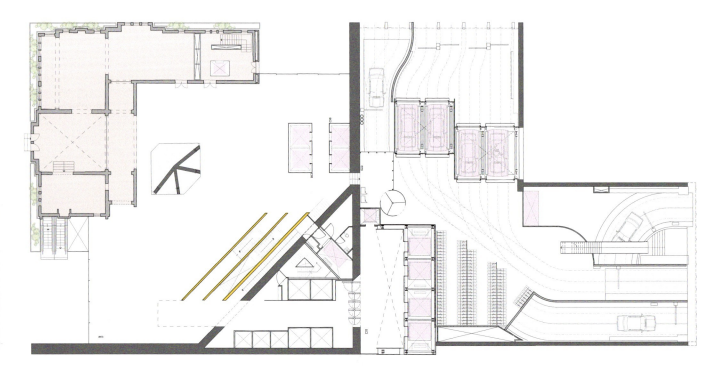

Ground Floor Plan
Grundriss Erdgeschoss

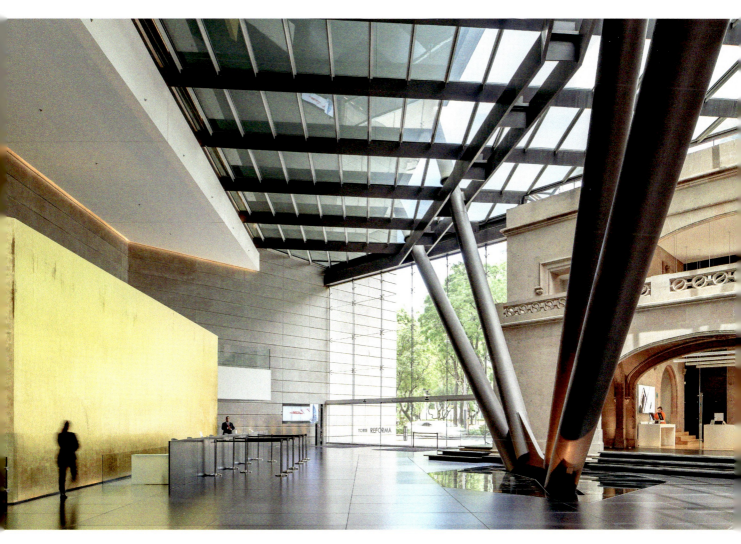

The foyer between the historic villa and the new structure serves as a public plaza. The golden colour of the walls behind the reception quotes the Mexican-German artist Mathias Goeritz.

Das Foyer zwischen Alt- und Neubau dient als öffentlicher Raum. Die goldene Farbe der Wände hinter dem Empfang zitiert den mexikanisch-deutschen Künstler Mathias Goeritz.

The highest building in the city, Torre Reforma towers above the historical villa without affecting its impact in the streetscape.
Als höchstes Gebäude der Stadt erhebt sich der Torre Reforma über der historischen Villa, ohne deren Wirkung im Straßenbild zu beeinträchtigen.

Benjamín Romano and und Peter Cachola Schmal

Benjamín Romano in Conversation with Peter Cachola Schmal
Mexico City, June 2018

Peter Cachola Schmal: So here we are, sitting in the middle of this amazing building which has an eight-year history. Is that a normal time span in Mexico for a building of this size?
Benjamín Romano: Well, we had a big problem with the authorities regarding the temporary relocation of the existing listed building on the site. It was difficult to convince them that our intentions were honest, that we really wanted to shift the historical house by 18 metres during the construction and put it back in its place afterwards – not to destroy it. And I have to say that it was difficult to get the financing straight.

PCS: Because you are not only the architect but the developer as well?
BR: Yes, exactly. The reason for the financial difficulties was that this building is rather different from the rest of the buildings that you can see in the surroundings. As you know, this tower has no columns. Then, we have no other foundations than the two walls that go all the way down. And we were saying to the financial partners that we were going to displace the existing house. So all of these ideas got the financial team concerned about the final success of the project. Because of those reasons, it took us eight years to realize this building. The construction process itself only took around three years.

Benjamín Romano im Gespräch mit Peter Cachola Schmal
Mexiko-Stadt, Juni 2018

Peter Cachola Schmal: Hier sitzen wir nun also in diesem erstaunlichen Gebäude, das eine achtjährige Entstehungsgeschichte hat. Ist das ein üblicher Zeitrahmen in Mexiko für ein Gebäude dieser Größe?
Benjamín Romano: Nun ja, wir hatten große Probleme mit den Behörden wegen der vorübergehenden Versetzung des denkmalgeschützten historischen Gebäudes auf dem Grundstück. Es war schwierig, sie davon zu überzeugen, dass wir es während der Bauarbeiten wirklich nur um 18 Meter verschieben und anschließend wieder zurückbewegen wollten – nicht etwa zerstören. Und ich muss sagen, es war nicht leicht, die Finanzierung zu bewerkstelligen.

PCS: Weil Sie nicht nur der Architekt, sondern gleichzeitig auch der Bauträger sind?
BR: Ja, genau. Die finanziellen Schwierigkeiten lagen darin, dass sich das Gebäude sehr von den Bauten in seiner Umgebung unterscheidet. Wie Sie wissen, ist dieser Turm stützenfrei. Außerdem gibt es kein weiteres Fundament außer den beiden Wänden, die tief herunterreichen. Und wir haben unseren Finanzpartnern gesagt, dass wir das bestehende Haus bewegen wollen. All diese Ideen haben den Finanziers Sorgen bereitet, ob das Projekt überhaupt erfolgreich sein kann. Deshalb hat es acht Jahre gedauert, das Gebäude zu realisieren. Der Bau selbst hat nur drei Jahre gedauert.

The two concrete walls reach 60 metres into the ground and act as foundations.
Die beiden Betonwände setzen sich als Fundamente 60 Meter tief in den Boden fort.

The Underground: Solid Foundation and Flood Risks

PCS: The interesting structural story is that this building consists basically of an angle of two walls and these two walls go down 60 metres.

BR: And in their full 1.2-metre width. They are embedded inside the rock. Remember that the city was built on a lake. The bottom of that lake is 23 metres beneath our building. So we opened the mud and the rock below and inserted the concrete walls. Thus, the building is supported by solid rock, not by the mud of the ancient lake which is such a big problem during earthquakes in Mexico City, as it is not solid, but moves.

PCS: And the other high-rises, how would they ground their foundations?

BR: They would do the same but not with walls. They have piles instead, one pile for each column, like in New York, and the piles should reach down 50–60 metres. That's how they normally do it. Since we don't use columns, we don't have those piles. So what we did was: we continued with the walls. And then we constructed nine underground levels. Because of the building codes, we had to supply parking spaces for 1100 cars. That's why we built this huge iceberg underneath the street. An astonishing fact is that the weight of the extraction of all this mud and soil is almost equal to the weight of the whole building. It's 76,000 tons of mud that we extracted from the site and which will most likely be used to build rural highways.

PCS: And what about the rainwater?

BR: We have a problem with rain in Mexico City, especially in the old part of the city. I always tell my students that you must build storage for rainwater because in the rainy season the city's drains are flooded. We did the same in this building to relieve the public drainage system. We need to learn more about this coexistence with nature and with water.

The space beneath the historical villa houses a food lounge. Its ceiling exposes the steel hinge located in the foyer.

Clusters and Supporting Structure

PCS: When we went through the building, we noticed that you hadn't divided it as usual, with one floor stacked on top of the other.
BR: Yes, we have 14 clusters of four floors each. The fourth floor is always a multi-tenant level. You can divide it for up to six tenants or just for one.

PCS: So the fourth floor of every cluster is self-contained. How about the remaining three?
BR: They are grouped around a garden, a triple-height patio. There's a structural reason for this: the concrete walls, that work as the façades, the foundations and as the structural system, are kind of stiff. So we needed to let them bend a little bit. Therefore, we incorporated openings of triple height in both of the walls – and the patios follow this rhythm. Imagine, with these cross-ventilated patios we can reduce the consumption of energy for air conditioning in the building by 25 percent. We did a study at Penn University in Pennsylvania and we noticed that this way, we could flush the heated, exhausted air from the inside and get back clean air at a lower temperature. So all of these factors end up dividing the building that way.

PCS: So you have the two concrete walls – and then you have the floors which are suspended from the walls via the diagonal steel braces.
BR: As you know, concrete is very good for compression and steel is very good for tension. So the steel braces pull back the stress, lift it up and then take it down through the concrete. In the end, the concept works like a woman's bra.
PCS: Which is also the origin of your family's business, isn't it?
BR: Well, my mother was a designer of intimate apparel and I certainly learned things from her.
PCS: This is a really interesting structural concept: a floor with a bra, and then the next floor with the next bra, multiplied 14 times.
BR: Plus the building core which is triangular.
PCS: …and shaped like an A.
BR: In my architectural scheme, I designed an A and I wanted to place the core into the triangular head of that A. I am convinced that as an architect you always have to comply with your architectural parti throughout the whole process. So I stayed with this parti till the end. You should have seen it in the construction process: an amazing tall structure without anything in it. Then we started adding the metal beams, the elevators and the stairs, the vertical ducts and the piping and everything the core needs – putting all of it into that triangular head of the A.

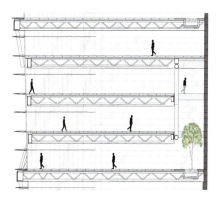

Cluster section
Schnitt eines Clusters

The elaborate structural system allows column-free floors, extensive open spaces and, not least, dramatic views from and of the building.
Das ausgefeilte Tragwerkskonzept ermöglicht stützenfreie Büroräume, großzügige Freiflächen und nicht zuletzt spannende An- und Ausblicke.

With two solid walls and a light third side, Torre Reforma creatively reinterprets the Aztec construction methods.
Mit zwei massiven Wänden und einer leichten, dritten Seite führt Torre Reforma die Bauweise der Azteken kreativ fort.

'Crumple zones' allow the otherwise stiff concrete walls to counterbalance the shocks during an earthquake. It was these openings that gave the building its nickname: 'Tetris Tower'.
Mithilfe der „Knautschzonen" gleichen die ansonsten steifen Betonwände die Erschütterungen während eines Erdbebens aus. Diese Öffnungen haben dem Gebäude den Spitznamen „Tetris-Turm" eingebracht.

Tectonic Mass

PCS: Your structural engineers, did they immediately go along with that idea?
BR: No.
PCS: What did they think?
BR: The original structural concept they gave me called for load-bearing vertical steel columns and just simulated the image of the concrete walls with cladding elements. And I thought that wasn't a wise idea because if you are going to use something in the structure, it should not be passive but should actively contribute.

PCS: So the engineers wanted a classical skin-and-bone structure, but you wanted a solid one?
BR: Yes, because that's the tectonic way of building in Mexico. If you analyze the ancient local architecture in Mexico, from Aztec times on, it was always clearly tectonic. Our ancestors knew that there has always been seismic activity here and will be forever. So we need to understand its effect if we want to build in a city such as Mexico City. That's why I insisted so much on having the solid concrete walls and having them act, too. They take a lot of compression stress out of an earthquake's effect.

PCS: When we come along Paseo de la Reforma and we see your building, we see a massive wall with sort of irregular holes, which is a very unusual view of a building in Mexico City. The others are mostly glass boxes. You oriented your glass façade to the park but the rear towards the city. What did the authorities say about a massive concrete façade facing a central part of town, the downtown in fact?
BR: They asked me the same, I explained it – and they loved it because it is a modern expression of the tectonic Mexican architecture. I don't think that the architecture has to be old, but that we should include vernacular architectural concepts in modern structures, since they contain knowledge learned through centuries of human development.

PCS: And the Aztecs, did they also build in the middle of the lake?
BR: Yes, but they built islands and lived on them. The Spanish didn't like that because there were a lot of infections through mosquitoes, so they decided to drain the lake. But the mud stayed – and we are on top of it.

Tektonische Masse

PCS: Waren Ihre Statiker von Anfang an von dem Konzept überzeugt?
BR: Nein.
PCS: Was hielten sie denn davon?
BR: Ihr ursprüngliches statisches Konzept sah vor, lasttragende vertikale Stahlstützen zu nutzen und die Anmutung von Betonwänden nur mit Verkleidungselementen zu simulieren. Ich hielt das für keine kluge Idee, denn wenn Sie etwas zur Konstruktion verwenden, sollte es nicht passiv sein, sondern aktiv zur Statik beitragen.

PCS: Die Statiker wollten also die klassische Skelettbauweise, Sie aber wollten eine massive?
BR: Ja, denn das ist die tektonische Bauweise Mexikos. Wenn Sie die historische Architektur Mexikos seit der Zeit der Azteken analysieren, war sie immer ganz klar tektonisch. Unsere Vorfahren wussten, dass es hier immer seismische Aktivitäten gegeben hat und immer geben wird. Wir müssen also verstehen, wie sie sich auswirken, wenn wir in Städten wie Mexiko-Stadt bauen wollen. Daher habe ich so sehr auf den massiven Außenmauern und ihrer Funktion beharrt. Sie nehmen einen Großteil der Druckbelastung bei einem Erdbeben auf.

PCS: Wenn man den Paseo de la Reforma entlangkommt und das Gebäude sieht, ist es eine massive Wand mit unregelmäßigen Löchern, was für Mexiko-Stadt ein ungewöhnlicher Anblick ist. Die anderen Bauten sind vorwiegend Glaskästen. Sie haben Ihre Glasfassade zum Park ausgerichtet und die Rückseite zur Stadt. Wie haben die Behörden darauf reagiert, dass Sie die massive Betonfassade einem zentralen Teil der Stadt, ja der Innenstadt, zugewandt haben?
BR: Sie haben mich dasselbe gefragt, ich habe es ihnen erklärt – und sie fanden es toll, weil es eine moderne Version der tektonischen Architektur Mexikos ist. Ich denke nicht, dass Architektur alt sein soll, aber dass wir traditionelle Architekturkonzepte in modernen Bauten aufgreifen sollten, da sie Wissen enthalten, das die Menschen über Jahrhunderte erworben haben.

PCS: Haben die Azteken auch schon in der Mitte des Sees gebaut?
BR: Ja, aber sie haben Inseln gebaut und darauf gelebt. Den Spaniern gefiel das nicht, weil es viele Infektionen durch Moskitos gab. Also beschlossen sie, den See trockenzulegen. Aber der Schlamm blieb – und wir obendrauf.

Sun Shading

PCS: The glass façade towards the park faces south. So does it heat up?
BR: No, because we included a lot of sun shades. Every two metres we built a fixed sun-shading device 1.2 metres wide. With the Penn University study, we were advised to use screening for the sun and it works very well. Additionally, towards the top of the tower, the storeys increasingly project outward, up to 14 metres compared to the ground floor, and provide additional shading to the façade below. In fact, if you go through the building, you will notice that nobody uses blinds to protect them from the sun because …
PCS: … the sun does not enter the glass?
BR: Exactly. So we don't have any heating effect from the sun. Normal glass façades are a problem here because the sun is very hot and you end up with blinds drawn all day long. So I don't think that glass buildings like in the US are a good concept for Mexico.

Verschattung

PCS: Die Glasfassade in Richtung Park weist nach Süden. Heizt sie sich also auf?
BR: Nein, denn wir haben viel Sonnenschutz eingebaut. Alle zwei Meter gibt es eine fixe Sonnenblende von 1,20 Meter Breite. Die Studie der Penn University empfahl uns, sie einzusetzen, und es funktioniert gut. Zusätzlich kragen die Geschosse nach oben hin immer weiter aus – bis zu 14 Meter gegenüber dem Erdgeschoss – und spenden so der Fassade darunter weiteren Schatten. Wenn Sie durch das Gebäude gehen, werden Sie feststellen, dass tatsächlich niemand Jalousien verwendet, weil …
PCS: … die Sonne nicht durch das Glas fällt?
BR: Genau. Deshalb haben wir auch keine Aufheizung durch die Sonne. Normale Glasfassaden sind hier ein Problem, denn die Sonne ist sehr heiß und am Ende hat man die Jalousien den ganzen Tag geschlossen. Deshalb halte ich Glasgebäude wie in den USA für keine gute Idee in Mexiko.

Aluminium sun shades allow natural lighting without heat gain in the strong Mexican sun.
Sonnenblenden aus Aluminium ermöglichen natürliche Beleuchtung ohne Aufheizen in der starken mexikanischen Sonne.

The upper floors steadily project outward to increase the floor space while also providing shade to the storeys below.
Die oberen Geschosse kragen zunehmend aus, um die Nutzfläche zu erhöhen und gleichzeitig den darunterliegenden Stockwerken Schatten zu spenden.

The conference rooms and auditorium can be reserved by the office tenants on an hourly basis. The terrace is open to everyone.

Die Konferenzräume und das Auditorium können von den Mietern der Büros stundenweise reserviert werden. Die Terrasse ist offen für alle.

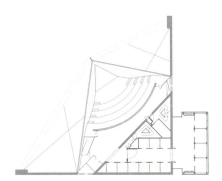

Floor plan level 23
Grundriss 23. Obergeschoss

Floor plan level 27
Grundriss 27. Obergeschoss

Floor plan level 47
Grundriss 47. Obergeschoss

Flows and Amenities

PCS: We are sitting on level 22 with the terrace behind and the auditorium on top of us. Why are they in this part of the building? Couldn't they have been on the top?
BR: No, they couldn't because to do a building like this you need to analyze the flow of everything. Talking about the flow of people, you cannot lift all the people to the top floor and then have them go down to their offices. That is why I placed the auditorium at half the height of the building and I divided the building in two parts: firstly, the commercial and sports areas plus the low-rise offices; secondly, the mid-rise and high-rise office floors. In between these two parts, I placed all the amenities: the terrace, the auditorium, the conference rooms and the cafe. So the low-rise office users can come up here and the mid- and high-rise users can come down. It's in the centre of the building. It could not be in another part.

PCS: Your concept of flows also led to the division of parking spaces. You put only half of the parking needed underground, but where does the other half go?
BR: The other half is in a smaller building attached to this tower that comprises 14 levels of a robotic parking system by the German company Wöhr. In my opinion, Mexico City will eventually develop a good public transportation system and then the cars will not be used anymore. Then this building will offer a lot of free space because of unused parking. Maybe I won't be alive at that time but I think that my task is to make a building for at least 100 years.
PCS: So you created a structure that can be used for some other purpose?
BR: Yes, that is the idea. Robotic parking needs a ceiling height of 1.8 metres and I built it 3 metres high. So when the parking is obsolete we can still use that space. I think it's my responsibility to consider things like this.

Wege und Treffpunkte

PCS: Wir sitzen in der 22. Etage, hinter uns liegt die Terrasse und über uns das Auditorium. Warum in diesem Teil des Gebäudes? Hätten sie nicht auch ganz oben liegen können?
BR: Nein, denn bei einem Gebäude wie diesem muss man alle Wege analysieren. Was die Wegeführung für Personen betrifft, so kann man nicht alle Menschen ins oberste Geschoss bringen und sie von da aus wieder zu ihren Büros herunterfahren lassen. Daher habe ich das Auditorium auf halber Höhe platziert. Ich habe das Gebäude in zwei Teile unterteilt: erstens den gewerblichen und Sportbereich plus die unteren Büroetagen, zweitens die Büroetagen in mittlerer und hoher Lage. Zwischen diesen beiden Teilen habe ich alle Treffpunkte platziert: die Terrasse, das Auditorium, die Konferenzräume und das Café. Die Nutzer des unteren Bereichs können also hier hinaufkommen, die aus dem mittleren und oberen Bereich hinunter. Es ist das Herzstück des Gebäudes und könnte daher auch nirgendwo anders liegen.

PCS: Ihr Wegekonzept hat auch zur Aufteilung der Parkbereiche geführt. Sie haben nur die Hälfte der benötigten Parkplätze unter die Erde gelegt. Wo ist der Rest?
BR: Die zweite Hälfte befindet sich in einem kleineren Gebäude neben dem Turm, in dem ein automatisches Parksystem der deutschen Firma Wöhr die Fahrzeuge auf 14 Etagen verteilt. Ich bin überzeugt, dass Mexiko-Stadt in Zukunft ein gutes öffentliches Verkehrssystem entwickeln wird und all die Autos nicht mehr nötig sein werden. Dann bietet dieses Gebäude aufgrund der ungenutzten Parkplätze sehr viel Raum. Vielleicht erlebe ich das nicht mehr, aber mein Ziel ist, Gebäude für mindestens 100 Jahre zu schaffen.
PCS: Also haben Sie eine Struktur entworfen, die anderweitig genutzt werden kann?
BR: Ja, das ist die Idee. Automatische Parksysteme benötigen 1,80 Meter Deckenhöhe, ich habe sie aber 3 Meter hoch gebaut. Wenn der Parkraum nicht mehr benötigt wird, kann der Raum also weitergenutzt werden. Es liegt in meiner Verantwortung, über solche Dinge nachzudenken.

The swimming pool on level 5 is part of an independent gym.
Das Schwimmbecken im 5. Obergeschoss ist Teil eines eigenständigen Fitnessstudios.

Architect and Developer

PCS: The quality of the finishing and the quality of the concept are exceptional. This has to do with you acting as the developer as well. What does it mean if the architect is also the developer? How does it work?

BR: What happened is that the people that I invited to invest with me agreed to do so as a capital investment. They are not planning to sell this building in order to have an immediate profit. They are going to keep it as a long-term investment for their families. That's a very important concept because it completely changes the scope of the building and also the scope of my work. I love things to remain functional. I do believe that good design is good business and if you make the things well at the beginning they will last forever. So that's why the investors that I invited accepted my proposal to invest in quality and the long-term.

PCS: So you find a site, you design a project, then you go to the authorities to get the building permit, and after that you invite others to join you in the realization of the building, is that right?

BR: That was the story of my first building, exactly as you are saying. In fact it is always the same group of investors now. After so many years in which I haven't failed they trust me and we invest in our projects together from the beginning.

PCS: And you design everything? I noticed that you know every detail.

BR: I am lucky to have a group of university students from my class, who are keen to work with me. Everything was designed by us.

PCS: That explains the quality of the detailing and the material. So in 20 years this will probably look very much like it is now?

BR: I hope so. In Spanish, we call this sort of investment *patrimonial,* which refers to the trust of your family. I have this vision that the investors keep their investments for their grandchildren. I believe it's a good concept because I admire Europe very much. I can go there and find a beautiful building built 500 years ago. Yes, it's renovated – yes, you can say whatever you want, but the building is there. In Mexico however, we have too many examples of one-dimensional modern architecture. And I think that those buildings are going to age badly. So I prefer to combine modern architecture with the principles of the original Mexican tectonic architecture.

Architekt und Bauträger

PCS: Die Qualität der Ausführung und des Konzepts ist außergewöhnlich. Das hat damit zu tun, dass Sie auch der Bauträger sind. Was bedeutet es, wenn der Architekt gleichzeitig als Bauträger fungiert? Wie funktioniert das?

BR: Die Menschen, die ich eingeladen habe, mit mir zu investieren, waren einverstanden, dies als Kapitalanlage zu betrachten. Sie planen nicht, das Gebäude zu verkaufen, um sofort Profit damit zu machen. Sie behalten es als langfristiges Investment für ihre Familien. Das ist sehr wichtig, weil es die Rahmenbedingungen des Gebäudes und meiner Arbeit völlig verändert. Ich liebe es, wenn Dinge funktionstüchtig bleiben. Ich glaube, dass ein guter Entwurf ein gutes Geschäft ist, und dass Dinge, die gut gemacht sind, ewig halten. Deshalb haben meine Investoren meinen Vorschlag akzeptiert, in Qualität und Langlebigkeit zu investieren.

PCS: Sie finden also das Grundstück, entwerfen das Projekt, gehen damit zu den Behörden, um es sich genehmigen zu lassen, und laden dann andere ein, sich an der Realisierung des Gebäudes zu beteiligen, richtig?

BR: Bei meinem ersten Bau ist es genau so abgelaufen, wie Sie es beschreiben. Tatsächlich ist es inzwischen immer dieselbe Gruppe von Investoren. Nach so vielen Jahren, in denen ich nie falsch lag, vertrauen sie mir und wir investieren von Anfang an gemeinsam in unsere Projekte.

PCS: Und Sie entwerfen alles selbst? Mir ist aufgefallen, dass Sie mit allen Details vertraut sind.

BR: Ich habe das Glück, dass eine Gruppe meiner Studenten gerne mit mir zusammenarbeitet. Alles wird von uns entworfen.

PCS: Das erklärt die Qualität der Details und des Materials. Also wird all dies in 20 Jahren vermutlich noch weitgehend genauso wie jetzt aussehen?

BR: Das hoffe ich. Auf Spanisch nennen wir diese Art der Investition *patrimonial,* was sich auf das Familienvermögen bezieht. Ich habe die Vision, dass die Investoren ihre Investitionen an ihre Enkel weitergeben. Ich halte das für ein gutes Konzept, denn ich bewundere Europa sehr. Ich kann dort ein wunderbares Gebäude finden, das vor 500 Jahren gebaut wurde. Natürlich ist es renoviert, und ja, Sie können sagen, was Sie wollen, aber das Gebäude ist da. In Mexiko hingegen haben wir zu viele Beispiele eindimensionaler moderner Architektur. Und ich glaube, dass diese Gebäude schlecht altern. Ich kombiniere moderne Architektur daher lieber mit den Prinzipien der ursprünglichen tektonischen Architektur Mexikos.

With its farsighted design, the building is meant to outlast at least the next 100 years.
Der vorausschauende Entwurf verspricht, dass das Gebäude mindestens 100 Jahre bestehen bleiben kann.

The lift lobbies are decorated with large-size photographs of the construction process.
Die Aufzugsvorräume zieren großformatige Fotos des Bauprozesses.

Benjamín Romano also designed the building's logo.
Auch das Logo des Gebäudes hat Benjamín Romano selbst entworfen.

Visit to the Prize Winner in Mexico City, June 2018   Reise zum Preisträger in Mexiko-Stadt, Juni 2018

At the architectural office Im Architekturbüro, **from left to right** von links nach rechts: **Benjamín Romano (Architect** Architekt**), Peter Cachola Schmal (Director** Direktor **Deutsches Architekturmuseum DAM), Silke Schuster-Müller (Head of Social Concerns** Leiterin Gesellschaftliches Engagement, DekaBank**), Maximilian Liesner (Curator and Coordinator IHA 2018** Kurator und Koordinator IHP 2018, **together with** zusammen mit **Peter Körner [not in this photo** nicht im Bild**])**

The International Highrise Award Internationaler Hochhaus Preis 2018

Take into Account the Dark to Tell the Light

With Torre Reforma, the International Highrise Award is being presented to a building that has a great deal to do with contemporary Mexican culture. Alexander Gutzmer, Editor-in-Chief of the architectural journal *Baumeister*, has lived in Mexico for the past two years. In this essay, he explains why the tower is symbolic on so many levels of present-day Mexico.

Anyone who, like me, watched the 2018 World Cup football match between Mexico and Germany in Mexico [fig. 1] was quickly confronted with a characteristic of the Mexican national soul that is frankly surprising: a propensity for fatalism. We know it: Mexico had the clearer strategy and rightly defeated the reigning world champion. Yet until the final whistle, the Mexicans could not believe their good fortune. 'Nothing's going to come of it anyway,' was the attitude at the start. And during the game, whenever the German team made even a half-serious offensive move: 'Oh God, now *Alemania* is taking the gloves off.' Finally, toward the end: 'Are we really winning? Us?' Only after the whistle was blown – and even then, after a few seconds of incredulous delay – did ear-splitting jubilation break out in the bars and restaurants.

In architecture, as in football, the country has little belief in itself. When I told my Mexican friends in confidence that this year Benjamín Romano, a Mexican architect, was to receive the International Highrise Award, no one would believe me. 'What – Mexico? What for?' No one could really imagine that the country was able to produce world-class architecture. Especially when, in this case, we were talking about a skyscraper – the epitome of a 'great' building.

Thus, it is all the more remarkable that with his Torre Reforma, Benjamín Romano not only placed a contemporary, bold and innovative 246-metre tower at the end of the skyline of Paseo de la Reforma [figs. 2, 3], but that he succeeded in taking the typology of the skyscraper still further – with an intervention which, in its roughness and conscious asymmetry, forms a counterpoint to the glossy bank capitalism of many major cities.

Romano demonstrates that Mexico City can – in its own way – be great. That fits a time when the metropolis is experiencing a revival in the international art and architecture scene. Many creative artists from Europe and the United States are currently moving to the city. Last year, our journal *Baumeister* devoted its entire July issue to the country of Mexico – and not least to its capital.

Das Dunkle mitdenken, um das Helle zu erzählen

Mit dem Torre Reforma erhält ein Gebäude den Internationalen Hochhaus Preis, das viel mit der mexikanischen Gegenwartskultur zu tun hat. Alexander Gutzmer, Chefredakteur der Architekturzeitschrift *Baumeister*, hat die vergangenen zwei Jahre in Mexiko gelebt. In diesem Essay erläutert er, warum der Turm auf vielen Ebenen so sinnbildlich ist für das Mexiko dieser Tage.

Wer, wie ich, im Sommer 2018 das WM-Fußballspiel zwischen Mexiko und Deutschland in Mexiko anschaute [Abb. 1], wurde schnell mit einer Eigenschaft der mexikanischen Volksseele konfrontiert, die eigentlich überrascht: dem Hang zum Fatalismus. Wir wissen es: Mexiko hatte die klarere Taktik und besiegte den Weltmeister verdient. Doch die Mexikaner konnten ihr Glück bis zum Schlusspfiff nicht fassen. „Das wird eh nichts", hieß es zu Beginn. Und während des Spiels, bei jedem halbwegs ernstzunehmenden deutschen Angriff: „Oh Gott, jetzt macht *Alemania* ernst." Gegen Ende schließlich: „Gewinnen wir wirklich? Wir?" Erst nach Abpfiff brach dann, immer noch ein paar ungläubige Sekunden zeitversetzt, in den Bars und Restaurants ohrenbetäubender Jubel aus.

Wie im Fußball, so ist auch in der Architektur der Glaube des Landes an sich selbst eher gebrochen. Als ich im mexikanischen Freundeskreis vertraulich berichtete, dass in diesem Jahr mit Benjamín Romano ein mexikanischer Architekt den Internationalen Hochhaus Preis erhält, glaubte mir keiner. „Wie – Mexiko? Für was denn?" Dass das Land architektonische Weltklasse hervorbringt, konnte und kann sich keiner so recht vorstellen. Zumal, wenn es dabei auch noch um ein Hochhaus geht, also den Inbegriff des „großen" Bauens.

Umso bemerkenswerter ist es, dass Benjamín Romano mit seinem Torre Reforma nicht nur einen zeitgemäßen, mutigen, innovativen 246-Meter-Turm ans Ende der Skyline des Paseo de la Reforma gesetzt hat [Abb. 2, 3]. Sondern, dass er es geschafft hat, die Typologie des Wolkenkratzers mit einer Intervention weiterzudenken, die in ihrer Rauheit und bewussten Asymmetrie ein Gegenstück zum gelackten Bankenkapitalismus vieler Großstädte setzt.

Romano zeigt: Mexiko-Stadt kann – auf eigene Weise – groß. Das passt in die Zeit, in der die Metropole ein Revival für die internationale Künstler- und Architektenszene erlebt. Viele Kreative aus Europa oder den USA ziehen momentan in die Stadt. Wir vom *Baumeister* haben im Jahr 2017 die gesamte Juliausgabe dem Land und nicht zuletzt seiner Hauptstadt gewidmet.

1
Mexican football fans on Paseo de la Reforma after the win against Germany in the 2018 World Cup
Mexikanische Fußballfans auf dem Paseo de la Reforma nach dem Sieg gegen Deutschland bei der WM 2018

2
(previous pages vorige Seiten)
3
Torre Reforma at the end of Paseo de la Reforma, which is lined by many important financial and cultural buildings
Torre Reforma am Ende des Paseo de la Reforma, der von vielen wichtigen Finanz- und Kulturbauten gesäumt ist

4
Augusto H. Álvarez; Alfonso González Paullada: Torre Latinoamericana, Mexico City
Mexiko-Stadt, 1948–1956

In a sense, with the construction of Torre Reforma, the city has come full circle – or more accurately, full axis – from Torre Latinoamericana [fig. 4] at the eastern end of the city centre, the entrance to the historic Old Town. This tower was completed in 1956 by Augusto H. Álvarez, with Alfonso González Paullada. The majority of the city's significant business buildings are located on this axis – including architecturally relevant structures such as the postmodern Stock Exchange building (1987–1990) by Juan José Díaz Infante [fig. 5] or the fascinatingly powerful Reforma 27 office building (2007–2010) designed by Alberto Kalach [fig. 6]. But it all began with Torre Latinoamericana. With a height of 204 metres including the antenna, this steel structure used to be the tallest building in Latin America.

Here, Álvarez formulated an optimistic Latino Modern style. Furthermore, he was carrying out pioneering work in practical construction: specifically, the tower withstood the severe earthquakes that struck the metropolis in 1957, 1985, 2012 and, most recently, 2017. As a result, the city's inhabitants developed a motto that is still valid today: in the event of an earthquake, 'safe' does not necessarily mean out on the street; instead, people might actually be safer in tall buildings – the very tall ones, on which structural engineers had been employed and were paid well for it.

This was also the case with Torre Reforma. For this reason, too, it represents a brilliant further development of the Álvarez tower. It is as earthquake-resistant as the earlier building; however, it does not hide its structural sophistication but extrapolates its architectural attitude from it. The curious and definitely undistinguished-looking openings in its concrete rear façade [fig. 7] do not merely illuminate the semi-public areas of the individual clusters, into each of which Romano grouped four storeys. Above all, they provide structural flexibility when the tower moves. And it does move – on the swampy subsoil of the megacity, which until a few centuries ago was a gigantic lakeland.

In gewisser Hinsicht schließt sich mit dem Torre Reforma der Kreis – oder man sollte besser sagen: die Achse – zum Torre Latinoamericana [Abb. 4] am östlichen Ende des Zentrums, am Eingang zur historischen Altstadt. 1956 stellte ihn Augusto H. Álvarez gemeinsam mit Alfonso González Paullada fertig. Auf dieser Achse liegen die meisten wesentlichen Geschäftsbauten der Stadt, darunter auch architektonisch Relevantes wie die postmoderne Börse (1987–1990) von Juan José Díaz Infante [Abb. 5] oder der faszinierend kraftvolle Bürobau Reforma 27 (2007–2010) von Alberto Kalach [Abb. 6]. Doch am Anfang stand der Torre Latinoamericana. Mit einer Gesamthöhe von 204 Metern inklusive Antenne war der Stahlbau damals das höchste Gebäude Lateinamerikas.

Álvarez formulierte hier eine optimistische Latino-Moderne. Darüber hinaus betrieb er baupraktische Pionierarbeit. Der Turm überstand nämlich die schlimmen Erdbeben, die der Metropole 1957, 1985, 2012 und zuletzt 2017 zusetzten. So entwickelten die Städter eine bis heute gültige Devise: Bei einem Erdbeben ist „sicher" nicht notwendig auf der Straße, sondern womöglich gerade in hohen Gebäuden – den ganz hohen, bei denen Statiker am Werk waren und anständig bezahlt wurden.

Das waren sie beim Torre Reforma ebenfalls. Auch deshalb bildet dieser die kongeniale Weiterentwicklung des Álvarez-Turms. Er ist erdbebensicher wie jener – versteckt aber seine statische Durchdachtheit nicht, sondern leitet aus dieser eine architektonische Haltung ab. Die seltsamen, so gar nicht repräsentativen Öffnungen in der rückwärtigen Betonfassade [Abb. 7] belichten nämlich nicht nur die halböffentlichen Bereiche der einzelnen Cluster, zu denen Romano jeweils vier Geschosse gruppiert hat. Sie sorgen vor allem für statische Flexibilität, wenn sich der Turm bewegt. Und das tut er auf dem sumpfigen Untergrund der Metropole, der bis vor Jahrhunderten eine riesige Seenlandschaft bildete.

5
Juan José Díaz Infante: Stock Exchange building Börse, Mexico City Mexiko-Stadt, **1987–1990** (middle and right Mitte und rechts)

6
Alberto Kalach: Reforma 27, Mexico City Mexiko-Stadt, 2007–2010

7
Inside view of openings in the concrete façade of Torre Reforma
Blick entlang der Öffnungen in der Betonfassade des Torre Reforma

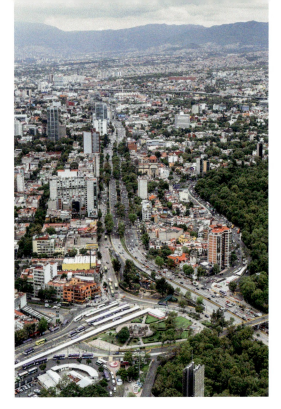

8
Traffic chaos in Mexico City as seen from Torre Reforma
Verkehrschaos in Mexiko-Stadt, gesehen vom Torre Reforma

9, 10
Pedro Ramirez Vazquez: Museo Nacional de la Antropología,
Mexico City Mexiko-Stadt, 1963–1964

11
David Chipperfield Architects: Museo Jumex, Mexico City
Mexiko-Stadt, 2009–2013

12
Torre Reforma's façade is characterised by alternating open
and closed elements.
Die Fassade des Torre Reforma wird bestimmt durch den
Wechsel von geschlossenen und geöffneten Teilen.

42   The International Highrise Award Internationaler Hochhaus Preis **2018**

Earthquakes, lakeland: in Mexico City, the experience of urbanity has always been a special one – and a precarious one as well. This metropolis of 20 million people has to struggle against the problems of a city that can never be completely pacified and in which drug cartels wreak havoc. The traffic is a living hell, in which arriving at your destination is always a matter of chance [fig. 8]. And up to now, the city has not been considered a must-see in the global architecture circus. Nevertheless, it has indisputably fascinating architectural substance to offer, including museums as the Museo Nacional de la Antropología (1963–1964, Pedro Ramirez Vazquez) [figs. 9, 10] and David Chipperfield's Museo Jumex (2009–2013) [fig. 11].

Overall, there is always something inherently feverish, erratic and restless about life in Mexico City. In this regard, the asymmetrical Torre Reforma, apparently winding around itself, seems to mirror this identity: with its two closed façades, it signals its function as a bastion. Its third side, however, opens up radically [fig. 12] – demonstrating that it is worth turning one's attention to this strenuous juggernaut and cultivating something akin to civic involvement within it.

Not the least of what stands against this are the massive divisions in Mexican society. The country is characterised by drastic differences and contradictions. Almost no other nation exhibits such a gap between the rich and the poor.

This very divide was the core issue for the winning candidate in Mexico's presidential election of 1 July 2018: Andrés Manuel López Obrador, the son of a small shopowner from the state of Tabasco. He was already making his third run for the office. His 'Morena' movement promised a politics for the poor, including unrealistic campaign promises that were not all thought through. But it worked. The people's desire for real change was great. 'AMLO', as he calls himself, met this desire with a mixture of populism, joviality and a swan song for elitist 'identity politics'.

Many people I spoke to during the campaign supported López Obrador. And they were not only the 'losers' of globalisation, who presumably acted in desperation. 'Mexico has enormous potential', the local manager of a European company said to me at an evening barbecue, 'but we are not taking advantage of this potential. This is due to our corrupt elites. The one who can dismantle this system should become head of government. And if anyone can, it is AMLO.'

Erdbeben, Seenlandschaft – die Erfahrung von Urbanität war in Mexiko-Stadt immer eine spezielle. Auch eine unsichere. Die 20-Millionen-Metropole hat mit den Problemen einer Stadt zu kämpfen, die nie ganz zu befrieden ist und in der Drogenkartelle ihr Unwesen treiben. Der Verkehr ist in einem Maße die Hölle, dass das Ankommen stets eine Lotterie darstellt [Abb. 8]. Und auch als Pflichtstation im globalen Architekturzirkus gilt die Stadt bisher eher nicht. Dabei hat sie unbestritten faszinierende Architektursubstanz zu bieten, unter anderem Museen wie das Museo Nacional de la Antropología (1963–1964, Pedro Ramirez Vazquez) [Abb. 9, 10] oder David Chipperfields Museo Jumex (2009–2013) [Abb. 11].

Insgesamt haftet dem (Er-)Leben von Mexiko-Stadt immer etwas Fiebriges, Unstetes an. Damit übernimmt der asymmetrische, sich um sich selbst zu winden scheinende Torre Reforma quasi Identität spiegelnde Funktionen. Weil er einerseits mit seinen beiden geschlossenen Fassaden die eigene Funktion als Trutzburg andeutet. Weil er sich dann aber auf seiner dritten Seite radikal öffnet und damit auch demonstriert, dass es lohnt, sich diesem anstrengenden Moloch zuzuwenden [Abb. 12] – und in ihm so etwas zu entwickeln wie bürgerschaftliches Engagement.

Dem stehen nicht zuletzt die massiven Spaltungen der mexikanischen Gesellschaft entgegen. Dieses Land ist von drastischen Unterschieden und Widersprüchen gekennzeichnet. Kaum eine Nation weist eine solche Kluft zwischen Arm und Reich auf.

Genau diese war das Kernthema des Siegers der Präsidentschaftswahl vom 1. Juli 2018, Andrés Manuel López Obrador, dem Sohn eines kleinen Einzelhändlers aus dem Bundesstaat Tabasco. Er kandidierte bereits zum dritten Mal. Seine Bewegung „Morena" versprach eine Politik für die Armen, inklusive unrealistischer und teils auch nicht durchdacht wirkender Wahlversprechen. Aber das kam an. Die Sehnsucht der Menschen nach echter Veränderung war groß. „AMLO", wie er sich nennt, bediente dieses Bedürfnis mit einer Mischung aus Populismus, Jovialität und dem Abgesang auf elitäre „Identitätspolitiken".

Viele Menschen, mit denen ich während des Wahlkampfs sprach, unterstützen López Obrador. Und es sind nicht nur Globalisierungsverlierer, denen man wahltaktische Verzweiflungsaktionen unterstellen könnte. „Mexiko hat ein Riesenpotenzial", sagte mir ein Manager eines europäischen Unternehmens bei einer abendlichen Grillparty. „Aber wir nutzen dieses Potenzial nicht. Das liegt an unseren korrupten Eliten. Es sollte derjenige regieren, der dieses System zerschlägt. Und wenn das einer kann, dann AMLO."

We will have to see how radical his policies turn out to be – and how he manages spatial developments in the country and its major cities. The challenges are great, and AMLO's messages in this regard during the campaign were not clearly defined. On the subject of Mexico City's airport, he has communicated a rather alarmingly populist stance. Together with the Mexican architect Fernando Romero, Norman Foster is planning a major new airport to the east of the city centre [fig. 13], not far from the present airport. From an architectural standpoint, this could become a huge success. Anyone who has had to travel through the current airport, with its two widely-spaced terminals, knows how urgently a new facility is needed. But AMLO wants to halt the project. In his opinion, too much private initiative is involved in the plan, and the connection between the former government, the business magnate Carlos Slim and Romero is too close. Slim, one of the world's wealthiest men, is financing the airport and is likely to want a share in its operation – and Fernando Romero is his son-in-law.

Nevertheless, Mexico needs this airport. And the planning is already quite advanced. If you fly into Mexico City today, you can look out of the window and recognise its topography. Along with the runways, the outlines of the complex – which is modelled on the 'X' in Mexico – are visible in the landscape. A large amount of money has already been invested in the project. From an economic perspective, stopping it would also be senseless.

Another plan of AMLO's seems more realistic in terms of infrastructure: expansion of the rail system. Today, all passenger transportation is carried out by aircraft, busses and private automobiles. Yet Mexico once had a railway network. Among other things, AMLO dreams of making the beaches of the Yucatán peninsula accessible via high-speed train. This makes sense. The states of Yucatán and Quintana Roo, which are located there, are in need of better

Man wird sehen müssen, wie radikal dessen Politik letztlich ausfällt. Und wie er die raumbezogene Entwicklung des Landes und seiner Metropolen steuert. Die Herausforderungen sind groß, AMLOs Wahlkampfsignale diesbezüglich waren nicht eindeutig. Ein eher beängstigendes Stück Populismus lieferte er in Sachen Flughafen Mexiko-Stadt. Norman Foster plant hier gemeinsam mit dem Mexikaner Fernando Romero einen neuen Großflughafen östlich des Zentrums [Abb. 13], nicht weit vom bisherigen Airport. Architektonisch könnte dies ein großer Wurf werden. Wer schon einmal den bisherigen Flughafen mit seinen zwei weit auseinanderliegenden Terminals nutzen musste, weiß, wie dringend ein neuer benötigt wird. Aber AMLO will das Projekt stoppen. Zu viel private Initiative steckt ihm darin und eine zu enge Verbindung zwischen der bisherigen Regierung, dem Unternehmer Carlos Slim und Romero. Slim, einer der reichsten Männer der Welt, finanziert den Flughafen und will ihn wohl auch mit betreiben. Und Fernando Romero – ist Slims Schwiegersohn.

Dennoch: Mexiko braucht diesen Flughafen. Und die Planungen sind bereits recht weit gediehen. Wer heute nach Mexiko-Stadt fliegt, kann beim Blick aus dem Fenster seine Topografie bereits erkennen. Die Umrisse, eine Anlehnung an das „X" aus „Mexiko", sowie die Landebahnen sind in der Landschaft angedeutet. Viel Geld wurde bereits investiert. Es wäre also auch ökonomisch sinnlos, das Vorhaben zu stoppen.

Ein anderer Plan AMLOs wirkt aus infrastruktureller Sicht nachvollziehbarer: der Ausbau der Schiene. Heute läuft der Personenverkehr vollständig über Flugzeuge, Busse und den privaten Autoverkehr. Dabei hatte Mexiko früher ein Schienennetz. AMLO schwebt unter anderem vor, die Strände der Halbinsel Yucatán per Hochgeschwindigkeitszug zu erschließen. Das ergibt Sinn. Die dortigen Bundesstaaten Yucatán und Quintana Roo brauchen eine bessere Anbindung an das Binnenland. Und grundsätzlich ist für das Flächenland Mexiko jeder Schritt in Richtung Schienenverkehr ein guter.

13
Foster + Partners; FR-EE: New International Airport, Mexico City
Mexiko-Stadt, 2014 (Rendering)

connections to the country's interior. And generally, given Mexico's vast territory, every step in the direction of rail traffic development is a good one.

But another thing is also clear: big-city architecture, as embodied by Benjamín Romano and his projects such as Torre Reforma and Torre Tres Picos (2009–2011) [fig. 14, 15], is not a subject close to López Obrador's heart. Nor will his core voters be the people who go to work on Paseo de la Reforma. They are more likely to go there now and then as part of a public protest, like the one that followed the 2006 elections. AMLO had lost in a close vote, and there was talk of election fraud. In response, his followers blocked Paseo de la Reforma for months, setting up a protest camp on the street; López Obrador was also there. The economic needs of the metropolis were irrelevant to him; however, the city's architecture (not yet including Torre Reforma) served as a backdrop for an anti-elitist demonstration.

Nevertheless, when one attempts to classify Torre Reforma in the context of Mexico's political and cultural debates, it actually does fit quite well – unlike many other high-rise buildings – into the programme of the Morena movement. Their campaign has repeatedly emphasised the value of Mexican working culture, Mexican handicrafts, etc. And Romano has certainly succeeded in creating a decidedly Mexican piece of culture.

In its very bulkiness, Torre Reforma is a reflection of contemporary Mexico. Its combination of transparency and almost Brutalist isolation mirrors the problematic truth: that this nation repeatedly founders on its own lack of transparency. In a sense, the building represents a farewell to a Modernism obsessed with transparency – a movement that has led to the construction of countless interchangeable glass and steel buildings, in Mexico City as elsewhere.

Klar ist aber: die Metropolenarchitektur, für die auch Benjamín Romano und seine Projekte wie der Torre Reforma oder der Torre Tres Picos (2009–2011) [Abb. 14, 15] stehen, stellt kein Herzensanliegen López Obradors dar. Seine Stammwähler werden auch nicht entlang des Paseo de la Reforma arbeiten. Sie kommen eher zu öffentlichen Protesten mal dorthin, wie nach der Wahl 2006. AMLO hatte knapp verloren, man sprach von Betrug. Also legten seine Anhänger für Monate die Reforma lahm und errichteten ein Protestcamp auf der Straße. López Obrador war dabei. Die ökonomischen Bedürfnisse der Metropole waren ihm egal, die Architektur der Stadt (damals noch ohne Torre Reforma) diente als Kulisse für die elitenkritische Inszenierung.

Wenn man aber etwas abstrakter versucht, den Torre Reforma in die politkulturellen Debatten Mexikos einzuordnen, dann passt er, anders als viele andere Hochbauten, durchaus zur Programmatik der Bewegung Morena. Diese betonte immer wieder den Wert der mexikanischen Arbeitskultur, des mexikanischen Handwerks usw. Und Romano gelingt es durchaus, ein dezidiert mexikanisches Stück Kultur zu schaffen.

Gerade in seiner Sperrigkeit spiegelt der Torre Reforma mexikanische Gegenwart. Seine Kombination aus Transparenz und geradezu brutalistischer Abschottung spiegelt die Problematik, dass dieses Land immer wieder an seinen eigenen Intransparenzen scheitert. Das Gebäude stellt in gewisser Hinsicht einen Abgesang auf den transparenzfixierten Modernismus dar, dessen Ideen auch in Mexiko-Stadt zu vielen austauschbaren Glas-Stahl-Bauten führten.

14, 15
L. Benjamín Romano: Torre Tres Picos, Mexico City Mexiko-Stadt, 2009–2011

Romano's handling of the existing building of 1929 also fits with this idea. Instead of hiding it in the new construction, he moved it temporarily and then returned it, all but freestanding, to its original position on the avenue [fig. 16]. It now serves as the tower's main postal address – and articulates the idea that the history of the country and the city need not necessarily be understood as a series of revolutions. With regard to the architectural community, its message is this: 'Here, a caste of change-drivers (architects) are showing respect for our city's roots.'

But what are these roots? What does this country stand for? Creative artists are currently grappling with this question. Fashion designer Carla Fernandez travels across the country searching out local weaving patterns and cuts of dresses. Celebrity chefs like Enrique Olvera or Jorge Vallejo work with local ingredients and the lore of the Maya. In Hollywood, directors such as Guillermo del Toro are establishing a specifically Mexican narrative voice.

Oscar winner del Toro also summed up the Mexican spirit in a nutshell. When asked why he always weaves elements of darkness and horror into his films, he replied simply, 'I'm Mexican'. He went on to explain that no one loves life more than the Mexican people. But this is also because they have a consciousness of death. As a creative artist, one has to 'take into account the dark to tell the light'.

Take into account the dark to tell the light – this is the perfect epic description of Torre Reforma: transparency and concrete. Light and shadow. Playful lightness and functional severity. The euphoric creation of forms – and one foot (or many metres of concrete) firmly planted in the muddy, repeatedly quaking earth of the metropolis, Mexico City.

Alexander Gutzmer is Editor-in-Chief of the architectural journal *Baumeister* and Editorial Director at the Munich-based media company Callwey. Gutzmer holds a doctoral degree in cultural studies and is a professor at the Quadriga University of Applied Sciences in Berlin. For the past two years, Gutzmer has lived in Mexico, where he was guest professor at the Universidad Tecnológico de Monterrey. His book *Die Grenze aller Grenzen. Inszenierung und Alltag zwischen den USA und Mexiko* (The Border of All Borders: Presentation and Daily Life Between the USA and Mexico) has recently been published by kursbuch.edition.

16
The historical villa in front of Torre Reforma was temporarily moved during the construction of the tower.
Die historische Villa vor dem Torre Reforma wurde während der Bauzeit des Turms vorübergehend verschoben.

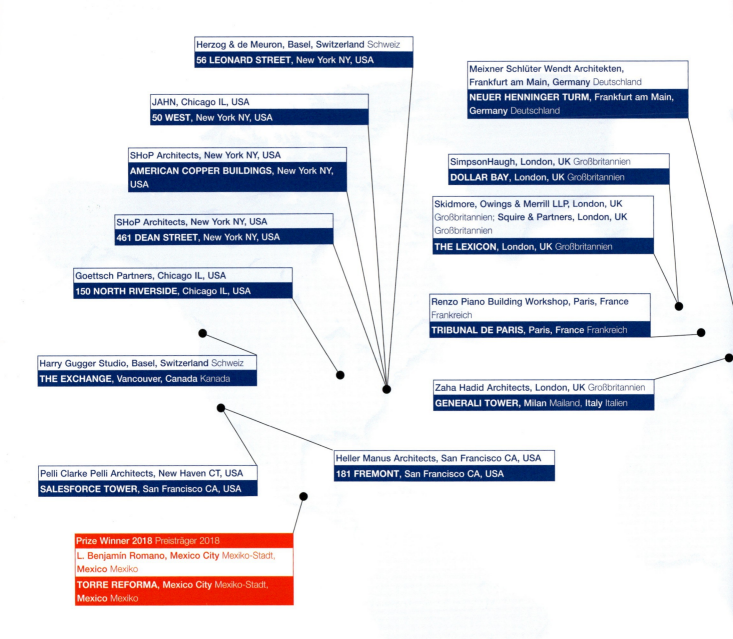

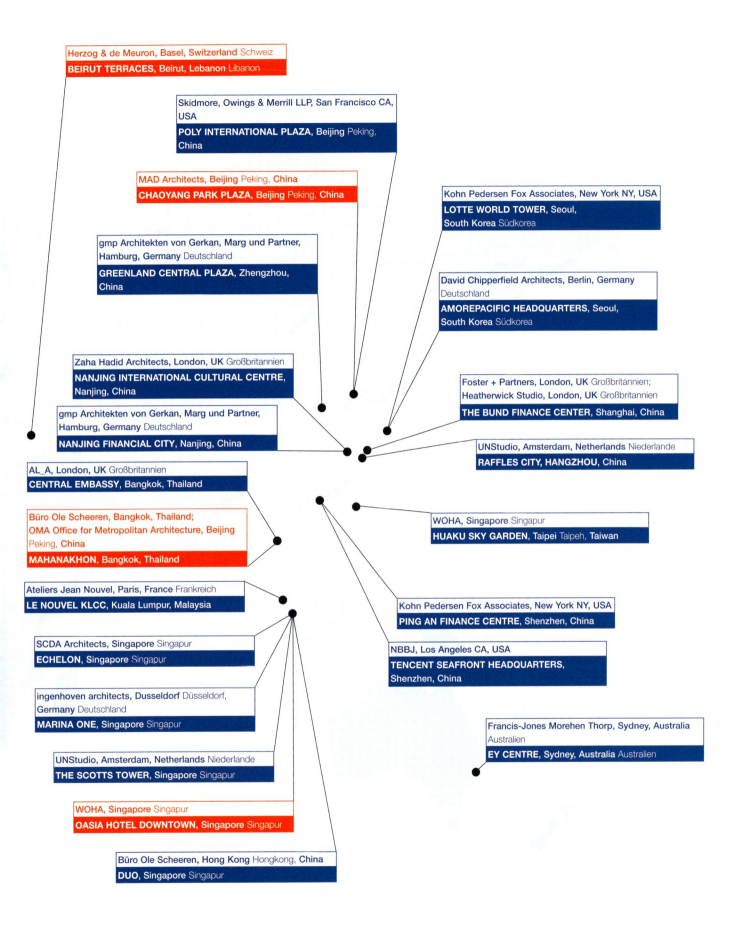

Finalist 2018

Büro Ole Scheeren;
OMA Office for Metropolitan Architecture
MAHANAKHON
Bangkok, Thailand

Architects Architekten Büro Ole Scheeren, Bangkok;
OMA Office for Metropolitan Architecture, Beijing
Peking, China
Client Bauherr PACE Development Corporation PLC
Structural engineers Tragwerksplanung Arup;
Bouygues Thai Ltd
MEP Haustechnik Aurecon Group;
Palmer & Turner Ltd

Height Höhe 314 m
Storeys Geschosse 77
Site area Grundstücksfläche 15 000 m²
Ground footprint Bebaute Fläche 6300 m²
Net floor area Nettogeschossfläche 112 800 m²
Structure Konstruktion Reinforced concrete
Stahlbeton
Completion Fertigstellung August 2016
Main use Hauptnutzung Mixed use comprising residential, hotel, retail and restaurants Mischnutzung aus Wohnen, Hotel, Einzelhandel und Restaurants

Sustainability
Nachhaltigkeit
Insulated glazing and natural ventilation at both smooth and pixel façades; pixels provide façade shading; rainwater harvesting; recycled grey water used for landscape irrigation
Isolierglas sowie natürliche Belüftung sowohl an ebener als auch an Pixel-Fassade; Verschattung der Fassade durch Pixel; Regenwassergewinnung; Nutzung recycelten Grauwassers zur Bewässerung der Grünanlagen

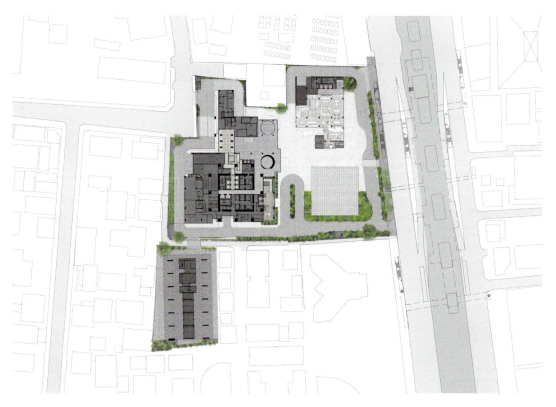

Siteplan
Lageplan

The winding pixelated ribbon dramatically cuts through the classical steel and glass cuboid.
Das gewundene Pixelband schneidet sich dramatisch in den ansonsten klassischen Stahl-und-Glas-Quader.

50 The International Highrise Award Internationaler Hochhaus Preis 2018

At 314 metres high, MahaNakhon is the tallest building in Thailand.
Mit 314 Metern ist MahaNakhon das höchste Gebäude Thailands.

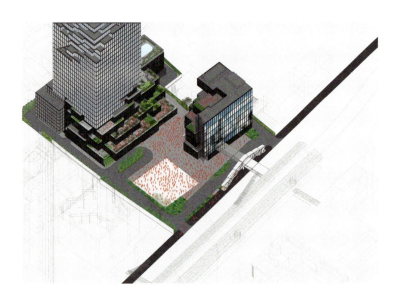

Axonometric view of the public plaza
Axonometrie des öffentlichen Platzes

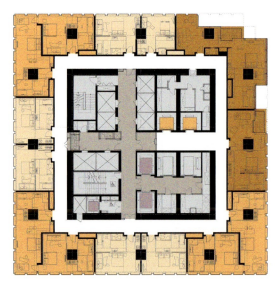

Hotel floor plan level 8
Hotel-Grundriss 8. Obergeschoss

After the Asian financial crisis of the late 1990s, Bangkok is now on its way to becoming a global city. With its name (meaning 'great metropolis'), its 314-metre height (making it Thailand's tallest building) and its distinctive pixel façade, the MahaNakhon project stands as a symbol of this new beginning. On the other hand, the pixelated sections of the façade could also be interpreted as representing the wounds that the countless new construction projects are inflicting on the city. Thailand's military government has been accused of demolishing traditional homes on a large scale, driving away street vendors and thereby robbing the original residents of their livelihood.

The pixelated ribbon winds around the entire height of the tower like a snake, spectacularly breaking up the otherwise consciously classical form of the steel and glass cuboid. But above and beyond this formal statement, the broken-up façade serves primarily to create terraces, balconies and freely hovering skyboxes. All of these offer unique views of the cityscape, which can be enjoyed by guests in the 155-room hotel that occupies the lower 20 storeys as well as by the residents of the 209 variously-sized serviced apartments in the 50 storeys above. The hotel rooms and apartments that face the smooth façade – and therefore do not benefit from the spaces created by the pixels – have been upgraded through the addition of innovative bi-fold windows which can be folded upwards, transforming the living room into a loggia space. Crowning the tower is a public observation deck with a 360° view as well as a double-height restaurant with an open-air rooftop bar.

Nach der asiatischen Finanzkrise Ende der 1990er-Jahre ist Bangkok inzwischen auf dem Weg, eine *global city* zu werden. Das Projekt MahaNakhon im zentralen Geschäftsviertel steht mit seinem Namen (auf Deutsch: „große Metropole"), seiner Höhe von 314 Metern als nunmehr höchstes Gebäude Thailands sowie seiner charakteristischen Pixelfassade stellvertretend für diesen Aufbruch. Andererseits können die verpixelten Teile der Fassade auch als Symbol für die Wunden gelesen werden, die die zahlreichen großen Neubauprojekte in die Stadt reißen. Der thailändischen Militärregierung wird vorgeworfen, in großem Stil traditionelle Wohnhäuser abzureißen, Straßenhändler zu vertreiben und so die ursprünglichen Bewohner ihrer Existenzgrundlage zu berauben.

Das Pixelband windet sich wie eine Schlange über die gesamte Höhe des Turms. Es löst damit die ansonsten bewusst klassische Form des Stahl-und-Glas-Quaders spektakulär auf. Über dieses formale Statement hinaus erzeugt die aufgebrochene Fassade aber vor allem Terrassen, Balkone und *skyboxes* genannte freischwebende Räume. Alle bieten einzigartige Ausblicke über die Stadt. Genießen können sie die Gäste des Hotels mit 155 Zimmern in den unteren 20 Geschossen sowie die Bewohner der 209 hochklassigen *serviced apartments* verschiedener Größe in den 50 Geschossen darüber. Die Hotelzimmer oder Wohnungen, die an die ebene Fassade grenzen und damit nicht von den durch die Pixel entstehenden Räumen profitieren, werden von innovativen Fenstern aufgewertet, die sich nach oben aufklappen lassen und so das Wohnzimmer in eine Loggia verwandeln. Bekrönt wird der Turm von einer öffentlichen Aussichtsplattform mit Rundumblick sowie einem Restaurant doppelter Raumhöhe mit einer Bar unter freiem Himmel.

Typical residential floor plan, levels 30–33
Wohnungsgrundriss Regelgeschosse 30–33

Typical residential floor plan, levels 60–65
Wohnungsgrundriss Regelgeschosse 60–65

The projections and recesses of the pixelated structure generate terraces, balconies and cantilevering skyboxes.
Die Vor- und Rücksprünge der Pixelstruktur erzeugen Terrassen, Balkone und freitragende *skyboxes*.

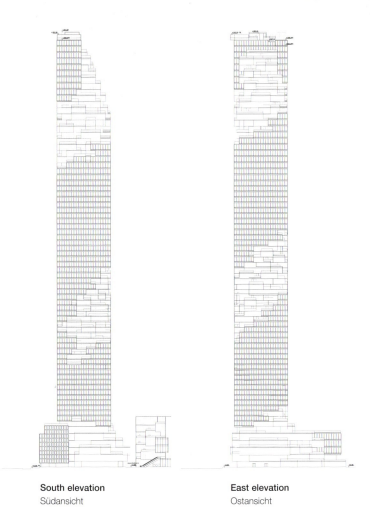

South elevation
Südansicht

East elevation
Ostansicht

The course of the pixelated ribbon along the tower's full height can be observed from different perspectives.
Aus verschiedenen Perspektiven lässt sich der Verlauf des Pixelbandes über die gesamte Höhe der Fassade verfolgen.

The base of the tower, housing the hotel lobby and amenities as well as restaurants and upmarket shops is designed not as a static podium but as a multi-level terraced landscape, rich in green. It picks up on the pixel motif and extends it horizontally, thereby creating a segue into the new public plaza in front. This serves as both an informal meeting place and as a venue for institutionalised cultural events. At its northern edge is a seven-storey cube, also part of the project, which houses additional shops and restaurants. On the sides facing the tower and the square, it likewise opens out into lavishly landscaped terraces. Further, it offers direct access to the adjacent Bangkok Skytrain station via a pedestrian bridge on its eastern side.

Having started the planning for MahaNakhon in his position as a partner of the Office for Metropolitan Architecture (OMA), Ole Scheeren founded his own firm in 2010 and took the project over. During further work on MahaNakhon, he opened a branch of his firm in Bangkok in 2015.

Jury statement

Jette Cathrin Hopp sees "an interesting twist to what is otherwise a classic typology by fragmenting and pixellating and thus slightly deconstructing the solidity of the overall appearance. At the same time, the building highlights a human scale by making the components legible in strategic positions."

In Sean Anderson's analysis, the building's shape "suggests a temporary breaking-down of iconicity and form" which Ina Hartwig identifies as "the cypher of the modern digital age".

Knut Stockhusen states: "The structural solution found, with the slight set-back of the outer columns to allow the levels to move inwards or outwards, is ingeniously integrated into the whole."

Der Fuß des Turms mit Hotel-Lobby und *amenities* sowie Restaurants und gehobenen Einkaufsmöglichkeiten ist nicht als starres Podium, sondern als mehrgeschossige, reichlich begrünte Terrassenlandschaft gestaltet. Sie greift das Pixelmotiv auf, erweitert es in die Breite und schafft so einen Übergang zum davor liegenden, neuen öffentlichen Platz. Dieser dient gleichermaßen als informeller Treffpunkt wie auch als Ort institutionalisierter Kulturveranstaltungen. Begrenzt wird er an seiner nördlichen Kante von einem 7-geschossigen Würfel, der ebenfalls Teil des Projekts ist und weitere Geschäfte und Restaurants beherbergt. Er öffnet sich gleichermaßen mit üppig begrünten Terrassen zum Turm und zum Platz. Darüber hinaus bietet er über eine Fußgängerbrücke einen direkten Zugang zur angrenzenden Station des Bangkok Skytrain.

Nachdem Ole Scheeren die Planung von MahaNakhon zunächst noch in seiner Funktion als Partner des Office for Metropolitan Architecture (OMA) begonnen hatte, gründete er im Jahr 2010 sein eigenes Büro und übernahm das Projekt. Im Zuge der weiteren Arbeit an MahaNakhon eröffnete er Ende 2015 auch eine Niederlassung in Bangkok.

Jurystatement

Jette Cathrin Hopp erkennt „eine interessante Variation einer ansonsten klassischen Typologie durch die Fragmentierung und Verpixelung, die Teile des blockhaften Gesamtbildes auflösen. Gleichzeitig unterstreicht das Gebäude ein menschliches Maß, indem es seine Bestandteile an strategischen Stellen ablesbar macht".

Sean Anderson analysiert, dass die Gestalt des Gebäudes „einen vorübergehenden Zusammenbruch des Ikonischen und der Form andeutet", was Ina Hartwig als „Chiffre auf das moderne digitale Zeitalter" interpretiert.

Knut Stockhusen stellt fest: „Die konstruktive Lösung ist intelligent in das Gesamtbild integriert. Denn die leicht zurückversetzten äußeren Säulen erlauben den Geschossen, nach innen oder außen zu rücken."

Finalist 2018

Herzog & de Meuron
BEIRUT TERRACES
Beirut, Lebanon Libanon

Architects Architekten **Herzog & de Meuron, Basel, Switzerland** Schweiz
Project architect Projektarchitekt **Stefan Marbach**
Architects of record Lokale Architekten **Khatib & Alami**
Clients Bauherren **DIB Tower SAL; Benchmark Development SAL**
Structural engineers Tragwerksplanung **Khatib & Alami; Arup**
MEP Haustechnik **Khatib & Alami; Arup**

Height Höhe **119 m**
Storeys Geschosse **26**
Site area Grundstücksfläche **4422 m²**

Ground footprint Bebaute Fläche **4273 m²**
Net floor area Nettogeschossfläche **60 000 m²**
Structure Konstruktion **Reinforced concrete** Stahlbeton
Completion Fertigstellung **June** Juni **2016**
Main use Hauptnutzung **Residential** Wohnen

Sustainability
Nachhaltigkeit
Seeking LEED Silver Certification; natural ventilation; shading by projecting floor slabs; water re-use; solar thermal panels on the roof; local micro-climates are created by a water garden on the entry level as well as by generous planted areas
LEED-Silber-Zertifizierung wird angestrebt; natürliche Belüftung; Verschattung durch auskragende Geschossplatten; Wasserwiederverwendung; Solarpaneele auf dem Dach; Wassergarten im Eingangsbereich sowie großzügige Begrünung sorgen für angenehmes Mikroklima

With ample outer spaces and a maximum of transparency, the building makes the most of the Mediterranean climate.
Mit weitläufigen Außenbereichen und maximaler Transparenz nutzt das Gebäude die Vorzüge des mediterranen Klimas.

Site plan
Lageplan

The area around Beirut's yacht harbour, with its palm-lined waterside promenade, still bears deep scars from the Lebanese Civil War (1975–1990) as well as the 2006 Israeli air strikes. This prestigious residential district is currently being redesigned according to an extensive master plan. One part of this plan is the spectacular residential tower, Beirut Terraces, constructed from concrete plates, layered and staggered on top of one another. With its white colour and dynamic form, the building clearly stands out from the surrounding grey highrises and, as an airy and light terraced landscape, embodies the hopes of this country ravaged by war. Beyond that, the building's different layers are intended to symbolise the periods in Beirut's turbulent history.

Das Quartier rund um Beiruts Yachthafen mit der von Palmen gesäumten Uferpromenade ist noch immer schwer vom libanesischen Bürgerkrieg (1975–1990) und den israelischen Luftangriffen von 2006 gezeichnet. Aktuell wird das renommierte Wohnviertel auf Basis eines umfangreichen Masterplans neu gestaltet. Bestandteil dieses Plans ist der spektakuläre Wohnturm Beirut Terraces mit seinen übereinander geschichteten und zueinander verschobenen Betonscheiben. Das Gebäude hebt sich mit seiner weißen Farbe und dynamischen Form deutlich von den grauen Hochhäusern der Umgebung ab und verkörpert als luftigleichte Terrassenlandschaft die Hoffnungen des kriegsversehrten Landes. Darüber hinaus sollen die verschiedenen Schichten die Epochen der turbulenten Geschichte Beiruts symbolisieren.

Fluent transitions between indoor and outdoor spaces offer residents an almost open-air lifestyle.
Fließende Übergänge zwischen Innen und Außen ermöglichen ein Wohnen fast wie unter freiem Himmel.

Beirut Terraces comprises 130 individually tailored apartments, ranging in size from 200 to 1000 square metres. Each home includes an additional outdoor space. The larger units extend over two storeys and boast terraces up to 450 square metres in size. Indoor and outdoor spaces merge into each other as the circumferential, floor-to-ceiling glazing and the consistent white colour of the concrete and Carrara marble surfaces blur the transitions. The inner living spaces and the surrounding outdoor areas can be used flexibly. Thus, the design is adapted to the city's moderate climate and fosters the open-air lifestyle that is typical of Beirut.

The mixture of various protrusions with accessible outer terraces results from the stacking of five different types of modular floor plates. These are supported by the inner service core as well as by columns set back from the edges. Through their projections and recesses, the single plates create interesting interplays between open spaces and retreats as well as between light and shadow. This play of light is further enhanced by the varying perforations in the overhangs. In addition to providing picturesque views of the sea to the north and the green boulevard to the east, the bands of windows ensure that plenty of daylight reaches the 3.4-metre-high living spaces, while the overhangs – at least 60 centimetres deep – protect them from strong direct sunlight.

Plant containers of various sizes bring vegetation to the balconies and establish private spaces vis-à-vis the adjacent units. At the same time, they improve the microclimate between the individual storeys. Moreover, these plantings, in combination with the extensively landscaped main entrance, are intended to make reference to the green of the palm trees on the neighbouring streets and simultaneously continue this motif in the vertical space. The interplay of architecture and nature is complemented by an extensive water garden in the main entrance area. Here, the spacious lobby creates a lively transition from the shops on the public ground floor to the private living areas located above. These are supplemented by a common observation terrace, a spa with a sauna, and a pool.

Beirut Terraces umfasst 130 auf die Bewohner individuell zugeschnittene Wohnungen von 200 bis zu 1000 Quadratmetern, die alle über zusätzlichen Außenraum verfügen. Die größeren Einheiten erstrecken sich über zwei Etagen und trumpfen mit Terrassen von bis zu 450 Quadratmetern Größe auf. Innen- und Außenraum verschmelzen zu einer Einheit, da die raumhohe Verglasung sowie die durchgängige Farbigkeit der weißen Beton- und Carrara-Marmor-Oberflächen die Übergänge verwischen. Die innen liegenden Wohnflächen und die umlaufenden Außenbereiche sind flexibel nutzbar. So reagiert der Entwurf auf das gemäßigte Klima und kultiviert das für Beirut typische Leben im Freien.

Den Mix aus verschiedenen Überständen mit nutzbaren Außenterrassen erzeugt die Stapelung von fünf Typen modularer Bodenplatten. Getragen werden diese durch den zentralen Versorgungskern und von den Kanten rückversetzte Säulen. Das Vor- und Zurückspringen der einzelnen Platten bewirkt interessante Wechselspiele zwischen Öffnung und Rückzug sowie Licht und Schatten. Verstärkt wird das abwechslungsreiche Lichtspiel noch durch die unterschiedlichen Perforationen in den Auskragungen. Neben den malerischen Ausblicken auf das Meer im Norden und den grünen Boulevard im Osten sorgen die Fensterbänder dafür, dass viel Tageslicht in die 3,40 Meter hohen Wohnräume fällt, während die mindestens 60 Zentimeter tiefen Überstände vor direkter Sonneneinstrahlung schützen.

Verschieden große Pflanzkästen begrünen die Balkone und erzeugen Privatsphäre zu den angrenzenden Wohnungen. Gleichzeitig verbessern sie das Mikroklima zwischen den einzelnen Ebenen. Außerdem soll die Begrünung, zusammen mit dem aufwendig bepflanzten Haupteingang, eine Beziehung zu den Palmen der benachbarten Straßen herstellen beziehungsweise diese in der Vertikalen fortführen. Komplettiert wird das Zusammenspiel von Architektur und Natur durch einen großflächigen Wassergarten am Haupteingang. Dort bildet die weitläufige Lobby einen lebendigen Übergang von den Geschäften im öffentlichen Erdgeschoss zu den darüber liegenden privaten Wohnbereichen. Ergänzt werden diese durch eine gemeinsame Aussichtsterrasse, ein Spa mit Sauna und einen Pool.

Overhanging floor plates provide the necessary shade.
Die überstehenden Geschossplatten spenden den nötigen Schatten.

Total volume
Gesamtvolumen

Setback
Rücksprung

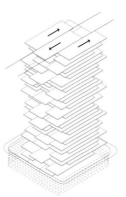
Shift slabs
Geschossplatten versetzen

Rotate differentiation
Umlaufende Fensterbänder

Support vertical structure
Vertikale Struktur stützen

Perforate edges
Kanten perforieren

Microclimate and privacy
Mikroklima und Privatsphäre

Concept diagram
Konzeptdiagramm

Ground floor plan
Grundriss Erdgeschoss

Floor plan level 20
Grundriss 20. Obergeschoss

60 The International Highrise Award Internationaler Hochhaus Preis 2018

Jury statement

"Beirut Terraces is a playful approach to the typology of the high-rise. The structural form defines an open principle which allows for a variety of alternatives within a defined set of rules, generating an expression that is as elegant as it is bold." (Jette Cathrin Hopp)

Ulrike Lauber praises: "Stacked, staggered and shifted, the residential layers create a seamless transition from the inside to the outside, protect from direct sunlight and offer welcoming spaces with a view. High-rise residences at their best." For Kai-Uwe Bergmann, too, the building is "a beautifully executed example of a new age of Middle Eastern high-rises designed to meet the region's unique challenges and climate".

Peter Cachola Schmal sees a connection to the visual arts: "Others have dreamt of a similar sculptural form before, such as the artist Thomas Demand, when he designed the sculpture of the International Highrise Award in 2003." This embodies a tower of stacked paper, representing the design process of a high-rise.

Jurystatement

„Beirut Terraces ist eine spielerische Interpretation der Hochhaustypologie. Die Struktur definiert ein offenes Konzept, das eine Vielzahl von Alternativen im Rahmen eines definierten Regelwerks zulässt und so ebenso Eleganz wie Mut ausdrückt." (Jette Cathrin Hopp)

Ulrike Lauber lobt: „Gestapelt, versetzt und verschoben schaffen die Wohnebenen einen grenzenlosen Übergang von innen nach außen, schützen vor direkter Sonne und bieten Aufenthaltsqualität sowie Ausblicke. Wohnen im Hochhaus ‚at its best'." Auch für Kai-Uwe Bergmann ist das Gebäude „ein wunderschön ausgeführtes Beispiel eines neuen Zeitalters nahöstlichen Hochhausbaus, das den speziellen Herausforderungen und dem Klima der Region standhält".

Peter Cachola Schmal sieht eine Verbindung zur bildenden Kunst: „Andere haben zuvor bereits solch skulpturale Formen erträumt, wie der Künstler Thomas Demand, als er 2003 die Skulptur für den Internationalen Hochhaus Preis entwarf." Diese stellt, in Anlehnung an den Entwurfsprozess eines Hochhauses, einen Turm aus gestapeltem Papier dar.

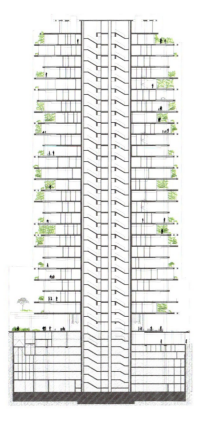

Section
Schnitt

Beside its aesthetic qualities, the water garden on the entry level functions as a natural air conditioning system. Neben seinen ästhetischen Qualitäten fungiert der Wassergarten im Eingangsbereich auch als natürliche Klimaanlage.

Finalist 2018

MAD Architects
CHAOYANG PARK PLAZA
Beijing Peking, China

Architects Architekten **MAD Architects, Beijing** Peking
Project architects Projektarchitekten **Ma Yansong; Dang Qun; Yosuke Hayano; Kin Li; Liu Huiying; Fu Changrui**
Architects of record Lokale Architekten **CCDI Group**
Client Bauherr **Smart-hero (HK) Investment Development Ltd**
Structural engineers Tragwerksplanung **CCDI Group**
MEP Haustechnik **Parsons Brinckerhoff Consultants Pte Ltd**

Height Höhe **142 m**
Storeys Geschosse **27**
Site area Grundstücksfläche **30 763 m²**
Ground footprint Bebaute Fläche **11 540 m²**
Net floor area Nettogeschossfläche **127 177 m²**
Structure Konstruktion **Reinforced concrete** Stahlbeton
Completion Fertigstellung **August 2017**

Main use Hauptnutzung **Mixed use comprising office, retail and residential** Mischnutzung aus Büros, Einzelhandel und Wohnen

Sustainability
Nachhaltigkeit
LEED Gold Certification; optimised use of natural lighting; tinted glass reduces solar gain; energy-efficient ventilation and filtration system draw a natural breeze indoors; pond at the base of the towers cools air naturally as it enters the interior during summer, reducing the building's overall temperature; thermally efficient façade composed of insulated glass with a thermal-break aluminum extrusion; standardized, cost-effective building materials; public areas with extensive greenery LEED-Gold-Zertifizierung; optimierte Nutzung natürlicher Beleuchtung; reduzierte Sonneneinstrahlung durch getöntes Glas; energieeffiziente Belüftungs- und Luftreinigungssysteme leiten frische Luft in den Innenraum; Teich am Fuß der Türme dient als Luftkühlung im Sommer und senkt die Gesamttemperatur des Innenraums; wärmeeffiziente Fassade aus Isolierglas mit einer Aluminium-Extrusion mit thermischer Trennung; standardisierte, kostengünstige Baumaterialien; öffentliche Bereiche mit üppiger Begrünung

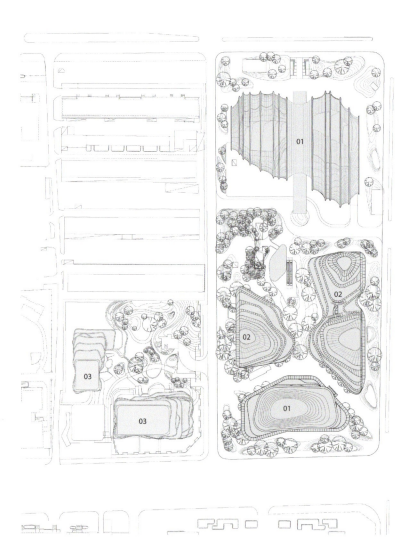 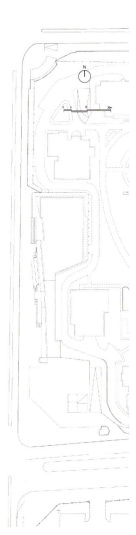

Site plan
Lageplan

01 Office
02 Retail
03 Residential
01 Büro
02 Einzelhandel
03 Wohnen

Curved glass and sharp-edged, rounded ridges determine the towers' amorphous shape.
Gewölbte Gläser und scharfkantige, abgerundete Grate bestimmen die amorphe Gestalt der Türme.

MAD Architects' design was inspired by traditional *Shanshui* painting.
Beim Entwurf haben sich MAD Architects von der traditionellen *Shanshui*-Malerei inspirieren lassen.

Depending on weather conditions, the two high-rises can convey the image of a picturesque hilly landscape or a mystic rock massif.
Je nach Wetterlage wirken die beiden Hochhäuser wie eine malerische Hügellandschaft oder wie ein mystisches Felsmassiv.

At the southern edge of the largest remaining park in Beijing's financial district, the ten mixed-use buildings of Chaoyang Park Plaza are distributed across an area of over 30,000 square metres. Their arrangement on the site appears quite random, almost like rock formations in nature. The two lofty, asymmetrical office towers rise on the banks of a lake like mountain peaks emerging from the water. Together with the lower-rise residential and commercial buildings, they define the in-between spaces, planted with pines and bamboo, which reference traditional Far Eastern landscapes. In this way, the green areas and water surfaces of the adjoining park are continued in the complex. The boundaries between nature and architecture are blurred as each merges into the other. Consequently, the public gardens are intended to serve visitors not only as meeting places, but also as spaces of calm retreat, away from the hustle and bustle of the city. Even the entrances to the underground shopping arcade, which connects several of the buildings to one another, are conceived as grottos.

For this project, MAD Architects took inspiration from the landscape images of traditional *Shanshui* painting (*shan* & *shui* = mountain & water). These are mostly drawn solely in black ink, and stem from the age prior to industrialisation. Consequently, they also represent the pristine, traditional China. The paintings are characterised by meandering, irregular lines that reflect the contours of the Chinese highlands, rather like a topographic map – a formal language that is consciously taken up in the amorphous, dark-glass building structures. Thus, the ensemble not only stands out clearly from its surroundings, it also symbolises a return to the Chinese sense of the organic. Through his designs Ma Yansong, head of MAD Architects, has not only criticised the ongoing urban development in Beijing – whose historic gardens have been forced to give way almost entirely to modern buildings – but he also aims to inspire the development of a contemporary, uniquely Chinese architectural language. He would like to see architecture and nature consistently perceived as an interactive whole. Despite the buildings' unusual shapes, it was possible to develop a cost-effective façade lining from unitized glass panels which were cold bent.

In addition to taking inspiration from *Shanshui* painting – which is especially evident to the Chinese public – the two distinctive office towers, in particular, evoke further associations. In bad weather, combined with the smog of the capital city, their sharp-edged forms and dark-coloured glass have an effect that is nearly as gloomy as Gotham City in the *Batman* films. At the same time, the curves between the dynamic ridges of the towers' peaks and of the shared, 17-metre-high atrium call to mind Antoni Gaudí's catenary arches.

Am südlichen Rand des größten noch verbliebenen Parks in Pekings Finanzdistrikt verteilen sich die zehn gemischt genutzten Gebäude des Chaoyang Park Plaza auf einer Fläche von über 30 000 Quadratmetern. Ihre Anordnung auf dem Gelände erscheint dabei eher zufällig, beinahe wie Felsbrocken in der Natur. Die beiden asymmetrischen Bürotürme ragen am Ufer eines Sees empor wie zwei Berggipfel aus dem Wasser. Gemeinsam mit den niedrigeren Wohn- und Geschäftsgebäuden definieren sie fließende, mit Pinien und Bambus bepflanzte Zwischenräume, die auf fernöstliche Landschaften zurückgreifen. Das Grün und die Wasserflächen des angrenzenden Parks setzen sich so in den Komplex fort. Die Grenzen zwischen Natur und Architektur verwischen, da sich beides ganz selbstverständlich ineinanderfügt. Dadurch sollen die öffentlichen Gärten den Besuchern nicht nur als Treffpunkte, sondern auch als ruhige Zufluchtsorte abseits der städtischen Hektik dienen. Selbst die Zugänge zur unterirdischen Einkaufspassage, die einige der Gebäude verbindet, sind als Grotten angelegt.

Bei dem Projekt ließen sich MAD Architects von den atmosphärischen Landschaftsbildern der traditionellen *Shanshui*-Malerei (*shan* & *shui* = Berg & Wasser) inspirieren. Sie sind meist nur mit schwarzer Tusche gezeichnet und stammen aus einer Zeit vor der Industrialisierung. Somit stehen sie für das ursprüngliche, traditionelle China. Charakteristisch sind sich schlängelnde, unregelmäßige Linien, die ähnlich einer topografischen Karte die Konturen des chinesischen Hochlandes wiedergeben – eine Formensprache, die die amorphen Baukörper aus dunklem Glas bewusst aufnehmen. Das Ensemble hebt sich so nicht nur optisch deutlich von seiner Umgebung ab, sondern verkörpert zugleich eine Rückkehr zum chinesischen Sinn für das Organische. Auf diese Weise kritisiert Bürochef Ma Yansong nicht nur die aktuelle Stadtentwicklung Pekings, dessen historische Gärten fast vollständig modernen Gebäuden weichen mussten, sondern will mit seinen Bauten auch die Entwicklung einer eigenen, zeitgenössischen chinesischen Architektursprache anregen. Architektur und Natur möchte er dabei stets als interagierende Einheit verstanden wissen. Für die Verkleidung der Fassadenflächen konnte trotz der ungewöhnlichen Form ein kosteneffizientes System aus standardisierten Glaspaneelen entwickelt werden, die kaltgebogen wurden.

Neben der insbesondere für das chinesische Publikum offensichtlichen Inspiration durch die *Shanshui*-Malerei wecken vor allem die beiden charakteristischen Bürotürme weitere Assoziationen. Ihre scharfkantige Form sowie das dunkle Glas wirken bei schlechtem Wetter im Smog der Hauptstadt beinahe so düster wie Gotham City aus den *Batman*-Filmen. Zugleich erinnern die Wölbungen zwischen den dynamischen Graten der Turmspitzen und des gemeinsamen, 17 Meter hohen Atriums an die Kettenbögen von Antoni Gaudí.

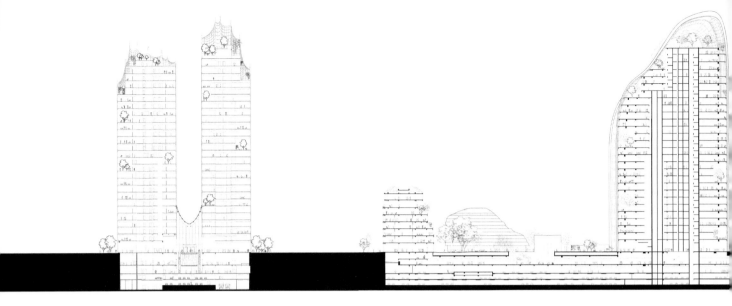

Sections
Schnitte

Ground floor plan
Grundriss Erdgeschoss

01 Office
02 Retail
03 Residential
04 Club
01 Büro
02 Einzelhandel
03 Wohnen
04 Club

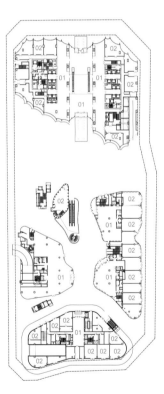

Typical floor plan
Grundriss Regelgeschoss

01 Office
02 Retail
03 Residential
01 Büro
02 Einzelhandel
03 Wohnen

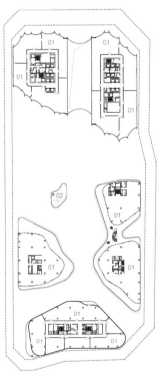

Jury statement

"Pleasant in scale and expression, this complex has a clear identity of its own, a design that is steeped in locality." (Ulrike Lauber) Sean Anderson continues: "Evoking Chinese historical landscapes and painting, the buildings integrate a continuity of surfaces, unique perspectives and a singular profile that challenge and intensify the potential of Beijing's rapidly expanding densities."

For Thomas Schmengler and Horst R. Muth the complex revokes seeming contradictions because it is "as highly unconventional as it is harmonious". Jette Cathrin Hopp draws the comparison to "the mass-produced, off-the-shelf high-rises typical of this part of the world" and concludes that Chaoyang Park Plaza positively stands out. Knut Stockhusen is astonished: "The curved façade segments were no doubt quite a challenge to design: Impressive!"

The greenery-stocked area serves as a recreational zone, at a time when open spaces in the city are diminishing due to ongoing population growth.

Finalist 2018

WOHA
OASIA HOTEL DOWNTOWN
Singapore Singapur

Architects Architekten **WOHA, Singapore** Singapur
Project architects Projektarchitekten **Wong Mun Summ; Phua Hong Wei**
Client Bauherr **Far East SOHO Pte Ltd**
Structural engineers Tragwerksplanung **KTP Consultants Pte Ltd**
MEP Haustechnik **Rankine & Hill Pte Ltd**

Height Höhe **199 m**
Storeys Geschosse **27**
Site area Grundstücksfläche **2311 m²**
Ground footprint Bebaute Fläche **2132 m²**
Net floor area Nettogeschossfläche **19 416 m²**
Structure Konstruktion **Reinforced concrete** Stahlbeton
Completion Fertigstellung **April 2016**
Main use Hauptnutzung **Hotel and offices** Hotel und Büros

Sustainability
Nachhaltigkeit
Green Mark Certification; replaces loss of green areas on site by more than ten times in amount and quality; high biodiversity through 21 species of façade creepers plus another 33 species of plants and trees as well as function as a habitat for small animals; over 40 percent share of open air space enables natural ventilation and lighting
Green-Mark-Zertifizierung; ersetzt das auf dem Grundstück ursprünglich vorhandene Grün durch mehr als das Zehnfache in Menge und Qualität; hohe Biodiversität durch 21 Arten von Kletterpflanzen plus weitere 33 Pflanzen- und Baumarten sowie Funktion als Habitat für Kleintiere; mehr als 40 Prozent Freiraumanteil ermöglichen natürliche Belüftung und Beleuchtung

Located in Singapore's dense city centre, this high-rise is a radical gesture in terms of aesthetics as well as of its use of space.
Im hoch verdichteten Stadtzentrum Singapurs ist dieses Hochhaus sowohl ästhetisch als auch vom Raumprogramm her eine radikale Geste.

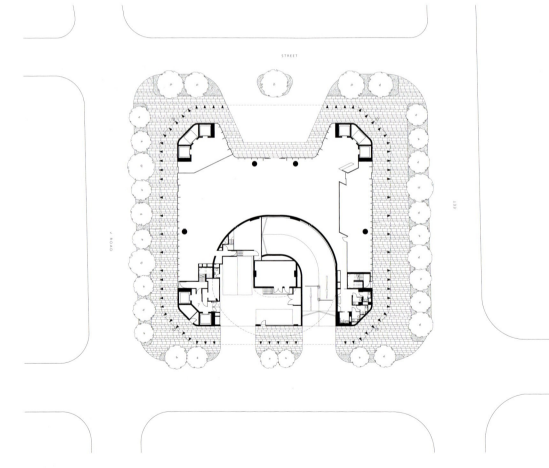

Site plan
Lageplan

Due to the extensive planting, the site now comprises more than ten times the amount of greenery it had before the start of construction.
Durch die umfassende Bepflanzung des Gebäudes weist das Grundstück nun zehnmal mehr Grün auf als vor dem Bau.

Over the past few years, through their innovative use of green and open spaces, WOHA have defined a new type of tropical skyscraper which, despite all its connection to nature, makes no secret of its machine aesthetics. They have already been honoured for this work, receiving the 2010 International Highrise Award for The Met in Bangkok. With the bold colours of their Oasia hotel and office tower, they are now forging a new path in terms of design.

The green of the plantings creates a striking contrast to the complementary red of the façade. The latter consists of thin, perforated aluminium panels over which the creepers grow and spread. In front of the window bands, where the panels appear only widely interspersed, the greenery remains restrained, but it is allowed to proliferate lavishly on the four windowless, fully enclosed corners, since each of these contains a service core. This design principle, which makes a central core unnecessary, allows for the inclusion of three sky gardens. With their pools and lush plant life, they provide hotel guests and office occupants with spaces for relaxation – over the entire surface of one storey and with unobstructed views in all four directions. They divide the building by grouping the storeys into three clusters and by extending upwards as atria through the full height of each. On each of the square floor spaces, the offices or hotel rooms occupy only an L-shape. This lends the façade a rhythm consisting of two open and two closed sides, whose orientation alternates with each cluster. The quantity of open space – more than 40 percent of the building's total volume – provides natural cross-ventilation and light to the offices and hotel rooms, which are arranged in double rows opening either to the outside or onto an atrium.

The first cluster contains 100 office spaces which, measuring between 39 and 48 square metres each, are intended for small businesses and are therefore not much larger than the 314 hotel rooms located in the second and third clusters. Housing the Club Rooms, the last of these grants its guests exclusive access to the adjacent atrium with an infinity pool. Two additional pools and a restaurant are available to all occupants on the roof terrace. Overhead, the green façade continues, crowning the building like an airy dome.

In the midst of the densely developed district of Tanjong Pagar, on the edge of Singapore's central business district, the Oasia Hotel Downtown thus creates what WOHA call a 'biophilic environment'. The economic efficiency of the tower has not had to suffer for this ecological diligence, but has in fact profited from it: not only because the aluminium grid used for the cladding was significantly less expensive than comparable panels made of glass or flat metal, but, above all, because the building's unique design has become the central marketing instrument for the hotel, resulting in high utilisation and profitable room rates.

Mit ihrem innovativen Einsatz von Grün- und Freiflächen haben WOHA im Laufe der vergangenen Jahre einen neuen Typus des tropischen Hochhauses definiert, der trotz aller Naturnähe keinen Hehl aus seiner Maschinenästhetik machte. Dafür wurden sie bereits 2010 mit dem Internationalen Hochhaus Preis für The Met in Bangkok ausgezeichnet. Mit den kräftigen Farben ihres Hotel- und Büroturms Oasia schlagen sie nun gestalterisch einen neuen Weg ein.

Das Grün der Bepflanzung setzt sich auffällig von der in der Komplementärfarbe Rot gehaltenen Fassade ab. Diese besteht aus dünnen, perforierten Aluminiumpaneelen, über die sich die Kletterpflanzen ausbreiten. Zurückhaltend bleibt das Grün vor den Fensterreihen, wo die Paneele nur lückenhaft eingesetzt sind; wuchern darf es an den fensterlosen, geschlossenen vier Ecken, da sich dort je ein Versorgungskern befindet. Dieses Konstruktionsprinzip, das einen zentral gelegenen Kern überflüssig macht, ermöglicht die drei *sky gardens*, die großzügig begrünt und mit Pools ausgestattet den Hotelgästen und Büronutzern zur Entspannung dienen – auf der gesamten Fläche je eines Geschosses und mit freiem Blick in alle vier Himmelsrichtungen. Sie gliedern das Gebäude, indem sie die Geschosse zu drei Clustern zusammenfassen und sich als Atrien jeweils über deren volle Höhe erstrecken. Auf der quadratischen Grundfläche des Gebäudes belegen die Büros oder Hotelzimmer nur eine L-Form. Dies führt zu einem Fassadenrhythmus aus je zwei geöffneten und zwei geschlossenen Seiten, deren Ausrichtung pro Cluster wechselt. Die mehr als 40 Prozent Freiraumanteil am Gesamtvolumen des Gebäudes ermöglichen eine natürliche Belüftung und Beleuchtung der doppelreihig angeordneten Büros und Hotelzimmer, die sich entweder nach außen oder zu einem Atrium öffnen.

Im ersten Cluster liegen die 100 Büros, die sich mit Größen von 39 bis 48 Quadratmetern an kleine Unternehmen richten und deshalb nicht viel größer sind als die 314 Hotelzimmer, die im zweiten und dritten Cluster folgen. Im letzteren befinden sich die Club-Räume, deren Gäste einen exklusiven Zugang zum angrenzenden Atrium mit *infinity pool* haben. Die Dachterrasse bietet zwei weitere Pools für alle Nutzer sowie ein Restaurant. Darüber setzt sich die begrünte Fassade nach oben fort und bekrönt das Gebäude wie eine luftige Kuppel.

Inmitten des dicht bebauten Viertels Tanjong Pagar am Rande des Geschäftszentrums von Singapur schafft das Oasia Hotel Downtown auf diese Weise ein, wie WOHA es nennen, „biophiles Umfeld". Die Wirtschaftlichkeit hatte unter dieser ökologischen Sorgfalt nicht zu leiden, sondern profitierte vielmehr davon: Nicht nur, dass das Aluminiumnetz als Fassadenverkleidung weitaus günstiger war als vergleichbare Paneele aus Glas oder flachem Metall – vor allem ist die einzigartige Gestalt des Gebäudes zum zentralen Marketinginstrument des Hotels geworden, das für hohe Auslastung und profitable Zimmerpreise sorgt.

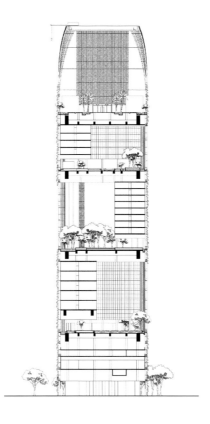

Section
Schnitt

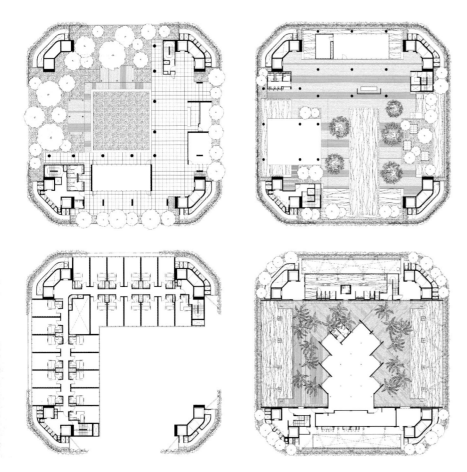

Floor plans
Levels 12 and 21
Levels 22 / 23 / 25 and 27
Grundrisse
12. und 21. Obergeschoss
22. / 23. / 25. und 27. Obergeschoss

Jury statement

Jury Chair Kai-Uwe Bergmann alludes to WOHA's innovations of the recent past when he states: "This high-rise continues WOHA's journey in blurring the lines of nature and architecture. The entire façade becomes an armature of the vegetation, creating a calming and shading veil." Knut Stockhusen observes: "This is a decidedly unique approach to an exoskeleton build without a central core. It allows maximum freedom of use, full functionality and voids in the central area."

Peter Cachola Schmal raves about the spatial qualities of the interior: "WOHA have managed to transfer the qualities of a resort into a downtown hotel and it works. To experience a great outdoor space fully cross-ventilated although that space lies within the core of the building volume and is thus protected from the frequent rains – is just unbelievable. This is the future for building high-rise structures in the tropics." And Jette Cathrin Hopp adds that also from the outside, "this building is a generous contribution to the urban fabric of Singapore."

Jurystatement

Der Juryvorsitzende Kai-Uwe Bergmann bezieht sich in seinem Statement auf die früheren Innovationen von WOHA: „Dieses Hochhaus schreibt die Reise WOHAs fort, auf der sie die Grenzen zwischen Natur und Architektur verwischen. Die gesamte Fassade wird zum Gerüst für die Vegetation und schafft so einen beruhigenden und Schatten spendenden Schleier." Knut Stockhusen merkt an: „Das Exoskelett ohne zentralen Kern ist ein einzigartiger Ansatz, der absolute Freiheit bei der Nutzung, volle Funktionalität und Freiräume im zentralen Bereich ermöglicht".

Peter Cachola Schmal ist vom Innenraum begeistert: „WOHA haben es geschafft, die Besonderheiten eines Resorts auf ein Innenstadthotel zu übertragen, und es funktioniert. Man erlebt einen rundum belüfteten Naturraum, obwohl man sich im Inneren eines Gebäudes befindet und damit geschützt ist vor den regelmäßigen Regenfällen – das ist einfach unglaublich. Dies ist die Zukunft des Hochausbaus in den Tropen." Jette Cathrin Hopp fügt an, dass auch das Äußere dieses Gebäudes „eine großartige Ergänzung des urbanen Gefüges von Singapur darstellt".

The building foregoes rentable hotel and office space in favour of generous sky gardens.

Zugunsten der Aufenthaltsqualität in den großzügigen *sky gardens* verzichtet das Gebäude auf weitere Quadratmeter vermietbarer Hotel- und Bürofläche.

Nominated Project 2018
Nominiertes Projekt 2018

AL_A
CENTRAL EMBASSY
Bangkok, Thailand

Architects Architekten **AL_A**, London, UK
Großbritannien
Project architect Projektarchitekt **Alice Dietsch**
Architects of record Lokale Architekten **Pi Design**
Client Bauherr **Central Retail Group**
Structural engineers Tragwerksplanung **Scott Wilson Kirkpatrick; Arun Chalseri Consulting**
MEP Haustechnik **MITR**

Height Höhe **176 m**
Storeys Geschosse **37**
Site area Grundstücksfläche **14 393 m²**
Ground footprint Bebaute Fläche **9342 m²**
Net floor area Nettogeschossfläche **145 000 m²**
Structure Konstruktion **Reinforced concrete**
Stahlbeton
Completion Fertigstellung **May** Mai **2017**
Main use Hauptnutzung **Hotel and retail** Hotel und Einzelhandel

Sustainability
Nachhaltigkeit
Zero waste and no offcut of aluminium façade material due to extrusion procedure; atria in retail spaces are naturally lit; green spaces on terraces; high-performance glass; footbridge connects to public transport
Verfahren der Extrusion zur Produktion der Aluminium-Fassadenverkleidung verursacht keinen Müll oder Verschnitt; Atrien inmitten der Verkaufsflächen natürlich beleuchtet; Grünflächen auf Terrassen; leistungsfähiges Glas; Fußgängerbrücke zu öffentlichem Nahverkehr

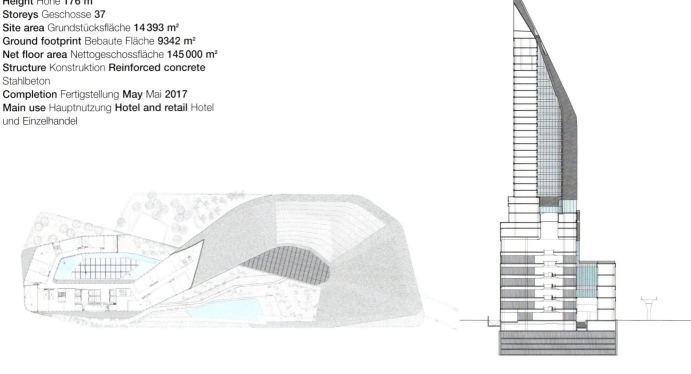

Floor plan level 16
Grundriss 16. Obergeschoss

Section
Schnitt

Situated in the former garden of the British Embassy, the Central Embassy project dominates the view of Bangkok's primary commercial artery, Ploen Chit Road. Rising from the luxurious shopping mall in its seven-storey, almost monolithic-looking plinth, the hotel tower extends upward in an undulating, asymmetric form. It encircles two atria, which subdivide the pedestal while simultaneously flooding it with natural light.

In the tradition of Thailand's intricate design patterns, the flowing facade is broken up by a moiré effect, achieved through cladding in specially-developed aluminium tiles. Their double surfaces reflect both the sky and the city, creating a fascinating play of light.

Gelegen im vormaligen Garten der Britischen Botschaft prägt Central Embassy das Erscheinungsbild von Bangkoks wichtigster Geschäftsstraße, der Ploenchit Road. Aus der luxuriösen Shopping Mall im 7-stöckigen, nahezu monolithisch anmutenden Sockel heraus entwickelt sich der Hotelturm in einer asymmetrisch geschwungenen Form. Diese umschließt zwei Atrien, die den Sockel natürlich belichten und zugleich gliedern.

In der Tradition aufwendiger thailändischer Muster wird die fließende Fassade durch einen Moiré-Effekt aufgelockert, der durch die Verkleidung mit speziell entwickelten Aluminiumkacheln erzeugt wird. Deren zweigeteilte Oberflächen reflektieren gleichzeitig den Himmel und die Stadt, wodurch das interessante Lichtspiel entsteht.

The International Highrise Award Internationaler Hochhaus Preis 2018　　75

Nominated Project 2018
Nominiertes Projekt 2018

Ateliers Jean Nouvel
LE NOUVEL KLCC
Kuala Lumpur, Malaysia

Architects Architekten Ateliers Jean Nouvel, Paris, France Frankreich
Project architects Projektarchitekten Mathieu Forest; Jean-François Winninger; Michel Calzada
Architects of record Lokale Architekten Arkitek MAA Sdn Bhd
Client Bauherr Wing Tai Malaysia Sdn Bhd
Structural engineers Tragwerksplanung P&T Consultants Pte Ltd; TY Lin International Sdn Bhd
MEP Haustechnik Jurutera Perunding Valdun

Height Höhe 200 m; 180 m
Storeys Geschosse 48; 43
Site area Grundstücksfläche 4896 m²

Ground footprint Bebaute Fläche 1269 m²
Net floor area Nettogeschossfläche 49 948 m²
Structure Konstruktion Reinforced concrete Stahlbeton
Completion Fertigstellung January Januar 2018
Main use Hauptnutzung Residential Wohnen

Sustainability
Nachhaltigkeit
About 70,000 plants of 243 species on the whole façade increase biodiversity and improve microclimate; drip irrigation system provides exact amount of water required; substrate of recycled local coconut shells keeps evaporation low; three vertical gardens
Etwa 70 000 Pflanzen 243 verschiedener Arten an der gesamten Fassade erhöhen die Biodiversität und verbessern das Mikroklima; Bewässerung per Tropfsystem liefert exakt nötige Wassermenge; Substrat aus recycelten lokalen Kokosnussschalen hält Verdunstung niedrig; drei vertikale Gärten

Typical floor plan
Grundriss Regelgeschoss

Section
Schnitt

The two towers of Le Nouvel KLCC are defined by the omnipresence of greenery. Emerging from approximately 10,000 planter boxes, an estimated 70,000 plants weave themselves along the grid that envelops the towers. The plants are watered by an automated system whose hoses are fed by water tanks located on the top and middle storeys. Vertical gardens – the trademark of garden architect Patrick Blanc, who is responsible for the landscaping – form the crown for both towers on the walls of the exposed building cores above the observation decks. The buildings are located directly opposite the twin Petronas Towers, which ranked as the tallest buildings in the world at the turn of the millennium. In dialogue with their shimmering metallic façades, the dominant green of Le Nouvel KLCC is intended to illustrate the dawn of a new era in high-rise construction – a change which is critically necessary in densely populated metropolitan centres like Kuala Lumpur.

Allgegenwärtiges Grün bestimmt die beiden Türme des Le Nouvel KLCC. Aus etwa 10 000 Pflanzkästen ranken sich ungefähr 70 000 Pflanzen entlang des Fassadengitters, das die Türme umschließt. Bewässert werden sie durch ein automatisiertes System, dessen Schläuche sich aus Wassertanks in den obersten und mittleren Geschossen speisen. Vertikale Gärten, Markenzeichen des verantwortlichen Gartenarchitekten Patrick Blanc, bekrönen beide Türme an den Wänden der freiliegenden Gebäudekerne über den Aussichtsplattformen. Direkt gegenüber befinden sich die Zwillingstürme der Petronas Towers, die um die Jahrtausendwende als höchste Gebäude der Welt galten. Im Dialog mit deren glänzend-metallischen Fassaden soll das dominante Grün selbstbewusst von der Zeitenwende im Hochhausbau zeugen, die für dicht besiedelte Metropolen wie Kuala Lumpur essenziell ist.

The International Highrise Award Internationaler Hochhaus Preis **2018** 77

Nominated Project 2018
Nominiertes Projekt 2018

Büro Ole Scheeren
DUO
Singapore Singapur

Architects Architekten **Büro Ole Scheeren, Hong Kong** Hongkong**, China**
Project architect Projektarchitekt **Claudia Hertrich**
Architects of record Lokale Architekten **DP Architects Pte Ltd**
Client Bauherr **M+S Pte Ltd**
Structural engineers Tragwerksplanung **BECA Carter Hollings & Ferner Pte Ltd; Buro Happold**
MEP Haustechnik **BECA Carter Hollings & Ferner Pte Ltd**

Height Höhe **186 m; 170 m**
Storeys Geschosse **50; 39**
Site area Grundstücksfläche **26 700 m²**
Ground footprint Bebaute Fläche **8000 m²**
Gross floor area Bruttogeschossfläche **160 350 m²**
Structure Konstruktion **Reinforced concrete** Stahlbeton
Completion Fertigstellung **October** Oktober **2017**
Main use Hauptnutzung **Mixed use comprising residential, offices, hotel and retail** Mischnutzung aus Wohnen, Büros, Hotel und Einzelhandel

Sustainability
Nachhaltigkeit

Public ground floor cooled entirely passively by captured and channelled wind; honeycomb shading system on the facades; direct access to metro station
Öffentliches Erdgeschoss vollständig passiv mit gezielt gelenktem Wind gekühlt; Wabenstruktur spendet der Fassade Schatten; direkter Zugang zu Metrostation

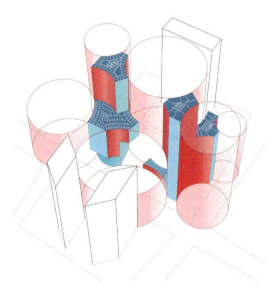

Conceptual sketch
Konzeptskizze

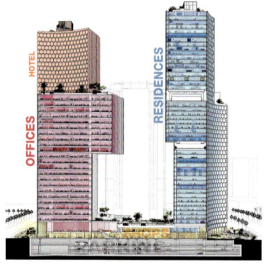

Section
Schnitt

The DUO building complex consists of a tower of office accommodation topped by a hotel, and a slightly higher residential tower housing 660 apartments. The idea for the design began with the newly landscaped open spaces. Their convex curves define the concave ground plan of the two towers. In this way, the complex is adapted to its environment and enhances the quality of this previously neglected location. The many paths leading through the greenery and past the businesses in the two-storey linking tract contribute to this effect. At the higher levels, the dramatic projections and recesses allow for the inclusion of additional private gardens, some with pools, as well as a public observation deck. The large-scale honeycomb structure provides shade to the façade, while evoking the image of a lively beehive.

Der Gebäudekomplex DUO besteht aus einem Büroturm mit darüber liegendem Hotel sowie dem wenig höheren Wohnturm, der 660 Apartments beherbergt. Am Anfang des Entwurfs standen die neuen, landschaftlich gestalteten öffentlichen Plätze. Deren konvexe Rundungen definieren die konkaven Grundrissflächen der beiden Türme. So passt sich der Komplex der Umgebung an und wertet den zuvor vernachlässigten Standort auf. Dazu tragen auch die vielen Wege bei, die durch das Grün und entlang der Geschäfte im zweistöckigen Verbindungstrakt führen. In der Höhe ermöglichen die dramatischen Vor- und Rücksprünge weitere private Gärten, zum Teil mit Pool, sowie eine öffentliche Aussichtsplattform. Die großflächige Wabenstruktur spendet den Fassaden Schatten und soll darüber hinaus auch das Bild eines quirligen Bienenstocks evozieren.

The International Highrise Award Internationaler Hochhaus Preis **2018**

Nominated Project 2018
Nominiertes Projekt 2018

David Chipperfield Architects
AMOREPACIFIC HEADQUARTERS
Seoul, South Korea Südkorea

Architects Architekten David Chipperfield Architects, Berlin, Germany Deutschland
Project architects Projektarchitekten Christoph Feiger; Hans Krause
Architects of record Lokale Architekten HAEAHN Architecture; KESSON
Client Bauherr Amorepacific Corporation
Structural engineers Tragwerksplanung Arup

Height Höhe 110 m
Storeys Geschosse 23
Site area Grundstücksfläche 14 500 m²

Ground footprint Bebaute Fläche 8700 m²
Gross floor area Bruttogeschossfläche 216 000 m²
Structure Konstruktion Composite Verbundbauweise
Completion Fertigstellung November 2017
Main use Hauptnutzung Office and public ground floor Büros und öffentliches Erdgeschoss

Sustainability
Nachhaltigkeit
LEED CS Gold Certified; orientation to the sun; utilisation of regional resources and craftsmanship; atrium and sky gardens create natural ventilation and admit daylight; diaphanous brise-soleil cladding
LEED-CS-Gold-Zertifizierung; Ausrichtung zur Sonne; Nutzung regionaler Ressourcen und Handwerksarbeiten; Atrium und erhöhte Gärten (*sky gardens*) schaffen natürliche Belüftung und Tageslicht; Verkleidung mit transparenten Brise Soleils

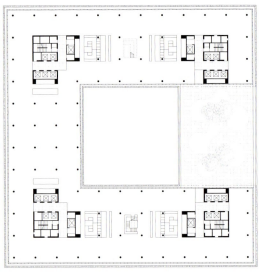

Floor plan level 16
Grundriss 16. Obergeschoss

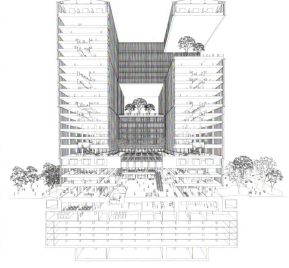

Sectional perspective
Perspektivischer Schnitt

The high-rise cube that houses the new corporate headquarters of Amorepacific, the country's largest cosmetics company, occupies a location between a large park on one side and the financial district – home to South Korea's tallest sky-scrapers – on the other. For the company's employees, the greenery of the park is continued in the generously proportioned sky gardens, which on three sides extend deep into the interior of the cube. The gardens are connected to the central atrium, which stretches upwards throughout the height of the building. The ground floor is accessible from all sides and dedicated entirely to public usage: it incorporates a museum, a library, a teahouse and shops. In addition, the atrium serves as a venue for cultural events.

Der Hochhauswürfel der neuen Firmenzentrale von Amorepacific, der größten Kosmetikmarke des Landes, nimmt eine Mittlerposition zwischen einem großen Park auf der einen und dem Finanzbezirk mit Südkoreas höchsten Hochhäusern auf der anderen Seite ein. Das Grün des Parks wird in den großzügig bemessenen *sky gardens* für die Mitarbeiter fortgeführt, die auf drei Seiten tief ins Innere des Würfels reichen. Sie sind mit dem zentralen Atrium verbunden, das sich in der Gebäudemitte über die volle Höhe erstreckt. Das von allen Seiten zugängliche Erdgeschoss ist mit einem Museum, einer Bibliothek, einem Teehaus sowie Geschäften ganz der öffentlichen Nutzung gewidmet. Das Atrium dient außerdem als Ort für kulturelle Veranstaltungen.

The International Highrise Award Internationaler Hochhaus Preis 2018

Nominated Project 2018
Nominiertes Projekt 2018

Foster + Partners;
Heatherwick Studio
THE BUND FINANCE CENTER
Shanghai, China

Architects Architekten **Foster + Partners, London, UK** Großbritannien; **Heatherwick Studio, London**
Architects of record Lokale Architekten **ECADI**
Client Bauherr **Shanghai Zendai Bund Int'l Financial Services Center Property Co, Ltd**
Structural engineers Tragwerksplanung **ECADI; Thornton Tomasetti**
MEP Haustechnik **ECADI; Mott McDonald**

Height Höhe **180 m**
Storeys Geschosse **39**
Site area Grundstücksfläche **45 472 m²**
Net floor area Nettogeschossfläche **426 073 m²**
Structure Konstruktion **Reinforced concrete** Stahlbeton
Completion Fertigstellung **March März 2017**
Main use Hauptnutzung **Office** Büros

Sustainability
Nachhaltigkeit
LEED Gold Certified Zertifizierung

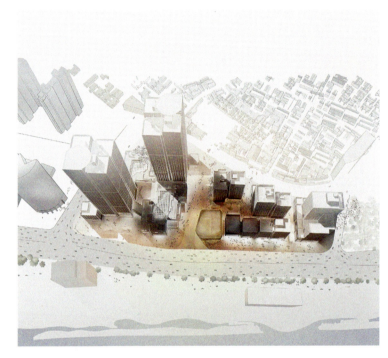

Perspective view
Perspektive

Site plan
Lageplan

The Bund – Shanghai's waterfront promenade – has been a centre for international trade since the middle of the nineteenth century, and owes its appearance to buildings of the colonial period. Foster + Partners and Heatherwick Studio have now given it a new end point. Along the riverbank, the height and rhythm of the staggered construction is oriented on the existing landmarks, while the two 180-metre-high office towers rise behind it. The eight buildings that make up the complex are grouped around a public square and visually connected to one another through their stone and bronze details. The towers stand out in particular for their roof terraces, helipads and lobbies with double-height ceilings. Located between offices, a hotel and luxury shops, the cultural centre – which serves as a venue for business functions as well as arts and cultural events – forms the heart of the new complex. Inspired by the open stages of traditional Chinese theatre, its façade is a moving curtain made up of bamboo-shaped steel pipes.

Die Uferpromenade The Bund ist bereits seit Mitte des 19. Jahrhunderts Zentrum des internationalen Handels und geprägt von Kolonialbauten. Ihr haben Foster + Partners und Heatherwick Studio einen neuen Abschluss verliehen. Entlang des Ufers orientiert sich die gestaffelte Bebauung in ihrer Höhe und Anordnung am Bestand, während sich die beiden 180 Meter hohen Bürotürme dahinter erheben. Die insgesamt acht um einen öffentlichen Platz gruppierten Gebäude werden formal durch Details in Stein und Bronze zusammengehalten. Die Türme zeichnen sich besonders durch Dachterrassen, Hubschrauberlandeplätze und doppelte Deckenhöhe der Lobbys aus. Mittig gelegen zwischen Büros, Hotel sowie Luxus-Shopping bildet das Veranstaltungszentrum, in dem neben kulturellen auch betriebliche Events stattfinden, das Herzstück des neuen Quartiers. Angelehnt an die offenen Bühnen traditioneller chinesischer Theater ist dessen Fassade ein beweglicher Vorhang aus bambusförmigen Stahlrohren.

The International Highrise Award Internationaler Hochhaus Preis 2018

Nominated Project 2018
Nominiertes Projekt 2018

Francis-Jones Morehen Thorp
EY CENTRE
Sydney, Australia Australien

Architects Architekten **Francis-Jones Morehen Thorp, Sydney**
Project architect Projektarchitekt **Richard Francis-Jones**
Client Bauherr **Mirvac Projects Pty Ltd**
Structural engineers Tragwerksplanung **BG&E**
MEP Haustechnik **Arup**

Height Höhe **155 m**
Storeys Geschosse **37**
Site area Grundstücksfläche **3147 m²**
Ground footprint Bebaute Fläche **1087 m²**
Net floor area Nettogeschossfläche **39 062 m²**
Structure Konstruktion **Reinforced concrete** Stahlbeton
Completion Fertigstellung **June** Juni **2016**
Main use Hauptnutzung **Office** Büros

Sustainability
Nachhaltigkeit
Green Star Certification: 6 Star Office Design v3 and 6 Star Office As-Built v3; Australia's first fully LED-lit building; closed cavity facade with automated timber blind system regulates light and heat and increases acoustic insulation; use of locally quarried sandstone and FSC and PEFC certified timber; post-completion data collection monitors performance (air quality, power and water usage, water recycling, façade performance, occupancy patterns, lift-use); cycling-friendly (307 bicycle spaces, 257 lockers, 65 showers); electric vehicle sockets
Green-Star-Zertifizierung: 6-Star-Office-Design-v3 und 6-Star-Office-As-Built-v3; Australiens erstes vollständig mit LEDs beleuchtetes Gebäude; Doppelfassade mit hölzernem, automatisiertem Rollosystem reguliert Licht und Wärme und verstärkt akustische Isolierung; Verwendung vor Ort abgebauten Sandsteins sowie FSC- und PEFC-zertifizierten Holzes; Datenerhebung während des Betriebs misst Leistung (Luftqualität, Energie- und Wasserverbrauch, Abwasseraufbereitung, Fassadenleistung, räumliche Auslastung, Aufzugnutzung); fahrradfreundlich (307 Stellplätze, 257 Schließfächer, 65 Duschen); Ladestationen für Elektroautos

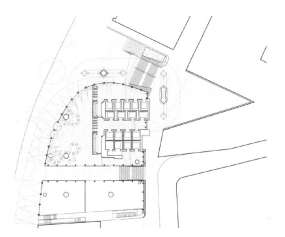

Site plan
Lageplan

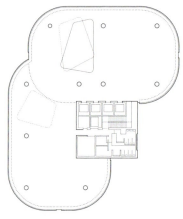

Typical floor plan
Grundriss Regelgeschoss

Between its grey steel and concrete neighbours, this building set on historic ground is intended to evoke the feeling of a wooden tower. To this end, the traditional material was crafted in rich detail and shaped over large areas using digital tools. Not only is it a striking design element in the foyer, but it is also used to great effect in the blinds that are made of natural timber slats. Encased in an airtight cavity between two layers of glass, these automatically supply the building with shade according to the position of the sun, while simultaneously providing a warm glow of colour both inside and out. In addition, the building, which is supported by two sculptural columns, defines a new public space. There, the building core is exposed and clad in sandstone that was quarried on the construction site. Archaeological findings from the site have been incorporated into the design of the outdoor space.

Zwischen seinen grauen Nachbarn aus Stahl und Beton soll das Gebäude auf historischem Boden den Eindruck eines Turms aus Holz erwecken. Dazu wurde der traditionelle Werkstoff mit digitaler Hilfe detailreich gestaltet und großflächig verarbeitet. Er ist nicht nur prägendes Gestaltungselement im Foyer, sondern kommt insbesondere bei den Jalousien aus hölzernen Lamellen deutlich zur Geltung. Luftdicht eingeschlossen zwischen zwei Schichten Glas verschatten diese, je nach Sonnenstand, automatisch das Gebäude und sorgen zugleich für eine warme Farbigkeit nach innen und außen. Darüber hinaus definiert der Bau, getragen von zwei skulpturalen Stützen, einen neuen öffentlichen Platz. Der hier freigelegte Gebäudekern ist mit auf dem Grundstück abgebautem Sandstein verkleidet. Archäologische Funde von der Baustelle wurden in die Gestaltung des Außenraums einbezogen.

The International Highrise Award Internationaler Hochhaus Preis **2018**

Nominated Project 2018
Nominiertes Projekt 2018

gmp Architekten von Gerkan, Marg und Partner
GREENLAND CENTRAL PLAZA
Zhengzhou, China

Architects Architekten gmp Architekten von Gerkan, Marg und Partner, Hamburg, Germany Deutschland
Project architects Projektarchitekten Meinhard von Gerkan; Stephan Schütz; Nicolas Pomränke
Architects of record Lokale Architekten Tongji Architectural Design (Group) Co, Ltd
Client Bauherr Zhongyuan RE Business Dept. of Shanghai Greenland Group
Structural engineers Tragwerksplanung schlaich bergermann partner GmbH
MEP Haustechnik Parsons Brinckerhoff Engineering Technology Co Ltd

Height Höhe 284 m
Storeys Geschosse 63
Site area Grundstücksfläche 54 490 m²
Ground footprint Bebaute Fläche 19 964 m²
Net floor area Nettogeschossfläche 746 202 m²
Structure Konstruktion Composite Verbundbauweise
Completion Fertigstellung December Dezember 2016
Main use Hauptnutzung Office Büros

Sustainability
Nachhaltigkeit
Natural ventilation via concealed openings in the façade profiles; close access to public transportation
Natürliche Belüftung aller Büros durch verdeckte Öffnungen in den Fassadenprofilen; gute Anbindung an den öffentlichen Nahverkehr

Typical floor plan
Grundriss Regelgeschoss

Floor plan level 60
Grundriss 60. Obergeschoss

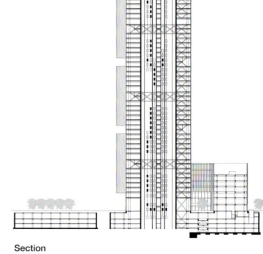

Section
Schnitt

Located in front of Zhengzhou's new east railway station, the symmetrical double towers form a gateway facing the city centre. Situated at the axis between a large square and a public park, the towers are among the central constructions of a completely new city district.

Two-storey sky lobbies incised into the façades on alternating sides create open spaces, offering a pleasant atmosphere even at lofty heights. They lend the twin towers their unique appearance, which is further underscored by their windmill-shaped ground plans.

At 4,000 square metres, the comparatively large storeys of this complex can be divided into small units for usage predominately as office space. While the topmost levels are reserved for exclusive use, public events such as art exhibitions or concerts take place in the adjacent, 15-storey-high atria.

Vor dem neuen Ostbahnhof Zhengzhous gelegen, bilden die spiegelsymmetrischen Doppeltürme ein Tor mit Blick zum Stadtzentrum. Am Übergang von einem großen Platz zu einem öffentlichen Park gehören sie zu den zentralen Bauten eines vollständig neuen Bezirks.

Zweigeschossige sky lobbys, die versetzt in die Fassaden eingeschnitten sind, schaffen selbst in luftiger Höhe noch Freiflächen mit angenehmer Aufenthaltsqualität. Sie verleihen den Zwillingstürmen ihr charakteristisches Erscheinungsbild, das durch die windmühlenförmigen Grundrisse noch verstärkt wird.

Die mit 4000 Quadratmetern vergleichsweise großen Geschosse des Komplexes lassen sich für die vorherrschende Büronutzung in kleine Einheiten aufteilen. Während die obersten Stockwerke einer exklusiven Nutzung vorbehalten sind, finden in den angrenzenden, 15-geschossigen Atrien beliebte öffentliche Veranstaltungen wie Kunstausstellungen oder Konzerte statt.

The International Highrise Award Internationaler Hochhaus Preis 2018

Nominated Project 2018
Nominiertes Projekt 2018

gmp Architekten von Gerkan, Marg und Partner
NANJING FINANCIAL CITY
Nanjing, China

Architects Architekten gmp Architekten von Gerkan, Marg und Partner, Hamburg, Germany Deutschland
Project architects Projektarchitekten Meinhard von Gerkan; Nikolaus Goetze; Marc Ziemons
Client Bauherr NFC Development Co Ltd

Height Höhe 130–200 m
Storeys Geschosse 30–46
Site area Grundstücksfläche 79 629 m²
Ground footprint Bebaute Fläche 18 600 m²
Net floor area Nettogeschossfläche 740 000 m²

Structure Konstruktion **Composite** Verbundbauweise
Completion Fertigstellung **September 2017**
Main use Hauptnutzung **Office** Büros

Sustainability
Nachhaltigkeit
Group of outer buildings: natural shading by vertical louvres prevents solar heat gain from east and west while allowing light from north and south to enter. Group of inner buildings: double façade with box-type windows including solar screening devices which are protected from the weather and can be individually operated
Äußere Gebäudegruppe: natürliche Verschattung durch Sonnenblenden verhindert Einstrahlung von starker Ost- und Westsonne und lässt gleichzeitig Licht aus Nord und Süd ein. Innere Gebäudegruppe: individuell bedienbarer, witterungsgeschützter Sonnenschutz in Doppelfassade mit Kastenfenstern

Siteplan
Lageplan

The first of two sections of the Nanjing Financial City complex comprises ten skyscrapers of varying heights for companies in the finance sector, as part of the extensive "Hexi New Town" urban expansion project. The outer edges of the site are defined by the three highest and the four lowest towers. The three medium-high towers are situated at the centre of the plot. Due to different energy saving approaches, the façades vary between the outer and inner group of buildings, thus providing vivacity to the complex. The areas between the buildings are generously landscaped with trees, creating a park-like atmosphere. Numerous seating areas and resting points are provided, especially along the banks of a small river, but also beside the many footpaths.

gmp is currently developing also the second phase of Nanjing Financial City, consisting of five additional towers – one of which will exceed 400 metres.

Der erste von zwei Teilen der Nanjing Financial City umfasst zehn unterschiedlich hohe Hochhäuser für Unternehmen der Finanzwirtschaft als Teil der umfangreichen Stadterweiterung „Hexi New Town". Die Außenkanten des Grundstücks werden von den drei höchsten und den vier niedrigsten Türmen markiert. Im Zentrum des Areals stehen die drei mittelhohen Türme. Lebendigkeit erzeugen dabei die Fassaden, die sich aus energetischen Gründen zwischen äußerer und innerer Gruppe unterscheiden. Die Zwischenräume der Gebäude sind mit vielen Bäumen parkähnlich angelegt. Besonders entlang eines kleinen Flusses, aber auch an den vielen Fußwegen befinden sich zahlreiche Sitzgelegenheiten und Ruhepunkte.

Der zweite Teil der Nanjing Financial City mit fünf weiteren Türmen, darunter einer von mehr als 400 Metern Höhe, wird derzeit ebenfalls von gmp geplant.

The International Highrise Award Internationaler Hochhaus Preis 2018

Nominated Project 2018
Nominiertes Projekt 2018

Goettsch Partners
150 NORTH RIVERSIDE
Chicago IL, USA

Architects Architekten **Goettsch Partners, Chicago**
Project architect Projektarchitekt **James Goettsch**
Client Bauherr **Riverside Investment & Development**
Structural engineers Tragwerksplanung **Magnusson Klemencic Associates**
MEP Haustechnik **Cosentini Associates**

Height Höhe **230 m**
Storeys Geschosse **54**
Site area Grundstücksfläche **7961 m²**

Ground footprint Bebaute Fläche **1755 m²**
Net floor area Nettogeschossfläche **114 000 m²**
Structure Konstruktion **Composite** Verbundbauweise
Completion Fertigstellung **January** Januar **2017**
Main use Hauptnutzung **Office** Büros

Sustainability
Nachhaltigkeit
LEED Gold Certified; connects and revitalizes a critical downtown parcel; very condensed core allows more than 75 percent of the site to be landscaped as a large public park; green roof
LEED-Gold-Zertifizierung; Revitalisierung und Anbindung eines schwierigen Innenstadtgrundstücks; äußerst kompakter und schmaler Kern ermöglicht großen, öffentlichen Park auf mehr als 75 Prozent der Grundstücksfläche; begrüntes Dach

Typical floor plan
Grundriss Regelgeschoss

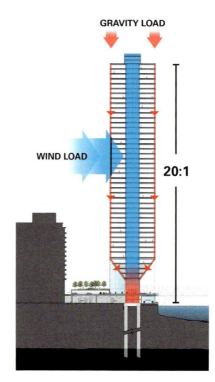

Section
Schnitt

At the edge of the Loop, the second largest business district in the United States, this property lay derelict for decades due to the fact that it was too tightly wedged between the Chicago River and the adjacent railway bridge. Complicating matters further, officials demanded that the riverbank promenade be extended as a prerequisite for building on the site. The solution was an extraordinarily narrow and compact building core. At ground-floor level, facing the water, the core is exposed, leaving space for the new promenade. Above this, where there were less spatial constraints, the support-free storeys project outward. On the opposite side of the building, a delicate glass wall descends from the overhanging storeys, enclosing the area underneath as a lobby. Through their vertical division into three cuboids, the end faces emphasise the slenderness of the tower. Here, the centre cuboid is slightly recessed to provide additional corner offices.

Am Rande des Loop, des zweitgrößten Geschäftsbezirks der USA, lag dieses Grundstück jahrzehntelang brach, weil der Chicago River und die angrenzende Eisenbahnbrücke es stark einengen. Zudem forderten die Behörden als Bedingung für eine Bebauung die Fortführung einer Uferpromenade. Die Lösung ist nun ein äußerst schmaler und kompakter Gebäudekern. Auf Erdgeschossniveau liegt er zum Wasser hin frei und schafft dadurch Platz für die neue Promenade. Darüber, wo sich die Raumsituation entspannt, kragen die stützenfreien Geschosse aus. Auf der vom Ufer abgewandten Seite ist von den auskragenden Geschossen eine filigrane Wand aus Glas abgehängt, die den Bereich darunter als Foyer umschließt. Die Stirnseiten betonen durch ihre vertikale Gliederung in je drei Quader die Schlankheit des Turms. Der mittlere Quader ist dabei leicht zurückversetzt, um zusätzliche Eckbüros zu ermöglichen.

Nominated Project 2018
Nominiertes Projekt 2018

Harry Gugger Studio
THE EXCHANGE
Vancouver, Canada Kanada

Architects Architekten **Harry Gugger Studio, Basel, Switzerland** Schweiz
Project architects Projektarchitekten **Harry Gugger; Alasdair Graham**
Architects of record Lokale Architekten **Iredale Group Architecture**
Clients Bauherren **SwissReal Group; Credit Suisse – Real Estate Fund International**
Structural engineers Tragwerksplanung **RJC Engineers**
MEP Haustechnik **Integral Group**

Height Höhe **131 m**
Storeys Geschosse **31**
Site area Grundstücksfläche **1870 m²**
Ground footprint Bebaute Fläche **1870 m²**
(**1200 m² new** neu)
Net floor area Nettogeschossfläche **40 200 m²**
Structure Konstruktion **Reinforced concrete** Stahlbeton
Completion Fertigstellung **November 2017**
Main use Hauptnutzung **Office and hotel** Büros und Hotel

Sustainability
Nachhaltigkeit
First LEED Platinum Heritage Conversion in Canada; shading by vertical mullions significantly reduces cooling load
Erste LEED-Platin-zertifizierte Sanierung eines denkmalgeschützten Gebäudes in Kanada; Verschattung durch vertikale Fenstersprossen reduziert die Kühllast beträchtlich

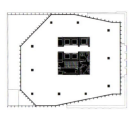 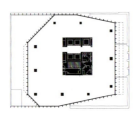
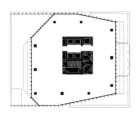 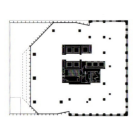

Floor plans levels
Grundrisse Obergeschosse
23–29 / 15–16
13 / 6–10

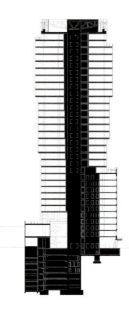

Section
Schnitt

Since Vancouver's city centre is located on a peninsula, the city endorses the construction of high-rises as a means of effective land usage. Nevertheless, defined visual axes which offer a view of the surrounding mountains and the ocean must remain unobstructed. As an inner-city densification project, The Exchange augments the landmarked Old Stock Exchange building, constructed in 1929, with an office tower, while preserving the historic structure and converting it into a hotel. The aluminium mullions, which reference the striking lesenes of the existing building, lend continuity to the design. While the lower storeys of the tower remain virtually invisible, allowing the old building to maintain its familiar presence in the streetscape, the tower gradually increases in width at its upper, more attractive levels.

Weil das Stadtzentrum von Vancouver auf einer Halbinsel liegt, befürwortet die Stadt den Hochhausbau als Mittel zur effektiven Landnutzung. Dabei müssen allerdings definierte Blickachsen, die Aussicht auf die umliegenden Berge und das Meer bieten, unangetastet bleiben. Als ein Projekt der innerstädtischen Nachverdichtung erweitert The Exchange das denkmalgeschützte ehemalige Börsengebäude (*Old Stock Exchange*) von 1929 um einen Büroturm, wobei der Altbau erhalten und zum Hotel umgebaut wurde. Für gestalterische Kontinuität sorgen die Fenstersprossen aus Aluminium, die die prägnanten Lisenen des Bestandsgebäudes aufgreifen. Während der Turm in den unteren Geschossen beinahe unsichtbar bleibt und dem Altbau weiterhin die gewohnte Präsenz im Straßenbild überlässt, wächst er in den oberen, attraktiveren Geschossen stufenweise in die Breite.

The International Highrise Award Internationaler Hochhaus Preis **2018** 93

Nominated Project 2018
Nominiertes Projekt 2018

Heller Manus Architects
181 FREMONT
San Francisco CA, USA

Architects Architekten **Heller Manus Architects,** San Francisco
Project architect Projektarchitekt **Jeffrey Heller**
Client Bauherr **Jay Paul Company**
Structural engineers Tragwerksplanung **Arup**

Height Höhe **244 m**
Storeys Geschosse **61**
Site area Grundstücksfläche **15 302 m²**
Ground footprint Bebaute Fläche **15 000 m²**

Net floor area Nettogeschossfläche **683 868 m²**
Structure Konstruktion **Steel** Stahl
Completion Fertigstellung **March** März **2018**
Main use Hauptnutzung **Office and residential** Büros und Wohnen

Sustainability
Nachhaltigkeit
LEED Platinum and REDI Certified; exoskeletal design reduces material needed; on-site cogeneration as well as grey water recycling; sawtooth design of curtain wall reduces solar gain LEED-Platin- und REDI-Zertifizierung; Exoskelett reduziert erforderliche Materialmenge; Kraft-Wärme-Kopplung und Grauwasser-Recycling vor Ort; schuppenartig überlappende Fenster verringern Aufheizen durch Sonneneinstrahlung

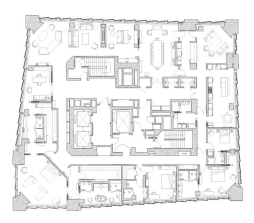

Floor plan grand penthouse
Grundriss großes Penthouse

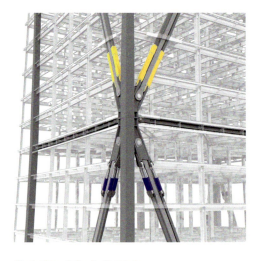

Illustration of shock absorbers
Illustration der Stoßdämpfer

The design for this building was crucially influenced by the prevailing seismic risk on the west coast of the United States. The foundation, which extends 80 metres into the bedrock, is the deepest in the region. Shock absorbers are built into the nodes of the steel exoskeleton, which can dissipate shocks caused by high winds or earthquakes. In addition, the building is the first in the US to be fully equipped with emergency evacuation elevators. Even though 181 Fremont is home to the highest-altitude residences in San Francisco, it is considered the safest private building in the region, and could be reoccupied promptly after a strong earthquake.

The offices in the lower storeys are separated visually from the residential units above them by a steel belt truss. This also allows for a column-free storey with joint-use facilities and a circumferential observation terrace, which also serves to dampen wind impact.

Der Entwurf für das Gebäude wurde maßgeblich durch die Erdbebengefahr an der US-amerikanischen Westküste geprägt. Das 80 Meter weit in den Felsboden reichende Fundament ist das tiefste der Region. In die Knotenpunkte des außen liegenden Stahltragwerks sind Stoßdämpfer eingebaut, die Erschütterungen durch starke Winde oder Erdbeben abfedern können. Im Notfall können darüber hinaus alle Aufzüge zur Evakuierung genutzt werden, was in den USA bisher einzigartig ist. Obwohl 181 Fremont die höchstgelegenen Wohnungen San Franciscos beherbergt, gilt es als sicherstes Privatgebäude der Region. Nach einem starken Erdbeben kann es umgehend wieder bezogen werden.

Optisch getrennt werden die Büros in den unteren Etagen von den darüber liegenden Wohnungen durch einen stählernen Fachwerkgürtel. Er ermöglicht zudem ein stützenfreies Geschoss mit gemeinschaftlich genutzten Bereichen und umlaufender Aussichtsterrasse, die wiederum die auftreffenden Winde bricht.

The International Highrise Award Internationaler Hochhaus Preis **2018**

Nominated Project 2018
Nominiertes Projekt 2018

Herzog & de Meuron
56 LEONARD STREET
New York NY, USA

Architects Architekten **Herzog & de Meuron, Basel, Switzerland** Schweiz
Project architect Projektarchitekt **Ascan Mergenthaler**
Architects of record Lokale Architekten **Goldstein, Hill & West Architects**
Client Bauherr **Alexico Group**
Structural engineers Tragwerksplanung **WSP Cantor Seinuk**
MEP Haustechnik **Cosentini Associates**

Height Höhe **253 m**
Storeys Geschosse **57**
Site area Grundstücksfläche **1162 m²**
Ground footprint Bebaute Fläche **990 m²**

Gross floor area Bruttogeschossfläche **37 975 m²**
Structure Konstruktion **Reinforced concrete** Stahlbeton
Completion Fertigstellung **July** Juli **2017**
Main use Hauptnutzung **Residential** Wohnen

Sustainability
Nachhaltigkeit
Less material used for slabs due to digitally optimized calculation; recycled industrial byproducts, slag and fly ash partly substitute cement and demand less water; fresh air intake through openable windows
Weniger Materialverbrauch für Geschossplatten durch digital optimierte Kalkulation; recycelte industrielle Abfallprodukte, Schlacke und Flugasche ersetzen teilweise Zement und benötigen weniger Wasser; Frischluftzufuhr durch zu öffnende Fenster

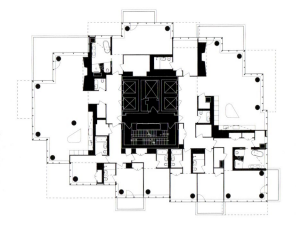

Floor plan level 44
Grundriss 44. Obergeschoss

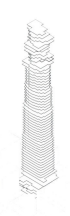   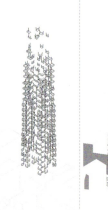

Concept diagram façade layering
Konzeptdiagramm Fassadenebenen

This residential tower, visually reminiscent of the popular 'Jenga' game, is located north of the World Trade Center and contains 146 stacked apartments, with individual floor plans ranging from 96 to 645 square metres and storey heights between 3.6 and just under 7 metres. On floor slabs that are staggered in relation to one another, with varying corners and projections, the individual spaces are arranged according to a pixel structure that works from the inside out. While the projections and recesses remain subtle in the tower's shaft, the upper and lower floors become more expressive, offering a wide variety of terraces and balconies as well as bay-window-like spaces. The result is not only a unique view from every room, but also the sense of urban density and a vertical neighbourhood provided by the presence of the surrounding storeys.

Der optisch an das Spiel „Jenga" erinnernde Wohnturm nördlich des World Trade Centers verfügt über 146 gestapelte Wohnungen mit individuellen Grundrissen zwischen 96 und 645 Quadratmetern sowie Geschosshöhen zwischen 3,60 und knapp 7 Metern. Auf zueinander verschobenen Bodenplatten mit variierenden Ecken und Auskragungen wurden die einzelnen Räume gemäß einer sich von innen nach außen entwickelnden Pixelstruktur angeordnet. Während die Vor- und Rücksprünge im Schaft des Turms subtil bleiben, werden sie in den unteren und oberen Etagen expressiver und bieten eine Vielzahl an Terrassen und Balkonen sowie erkerähnlichen Räumen. Somit entstehen nicht nur besondere Ausblicke aus jedem Raum, sondern durch die Präsenz der umliegenden Geschosse gleichzeitig ein Gefühl von vertikaler Nachbarschaft und städtischer Dichte.

The International Highrise Award Internationaler Hochhaus Preis 2018

Nominated Project 2018
Nominiertes Projekt 2018

ingenhoven architects
MARINA ONE
Singapore Singapur

Architects Architekten **ingenhoven architects, Dusseldorf** Düsseldorf, **Germany** Deutschland
Project architects Projektarchitekten **Christoph Ingenhoven; Martin Reuter; Olaf Kluge**
Architects of record Lokale Architekten **architects 61**
Client Bauherr **M+S Pte Ltd Singapore**
Structural engineers Tragwerksplanung **BECA Carter Hollings & Ferner**
MEP Haustechnik **BECA Carter Hollings & Ferner**

Height Höhe **237 m; 145 m**
Storeys Geschosse **30; 34**
Site area Grundstücksfläche **26 200 m²**
Ground footprint Bebaute Fläche **11 060 m²**
Gross floor area Bruttogeschossfläche **400 000 m²**
Structure Konstruktion **Reinforced concrete** Stahlbeton
Completion Fertigstellung **December** Dezember **2017**
Main use Hauptnutzung **Office and residential** Büros und Wohnen

Sustainability
Nachhaltigkeit
Green Mark Platinum and LEED Platinum Certified; natural ventilation of the complex; natural cross ventilation in all apartments; more than 350 plant species in the Green Heart; rainwater collected from the multiple roofs, terraces and façade used for irrigation; mesh louvres provide shading while maintaining airflow and influx of daylight; glazing that reduces solar radiation into the building; photovoltaic cells on the rooftop; bicycle parking facilities and electric vehicle charging stations; direct connections to several subway lines and bus stops
Green-Mark-Platin- und LEED-Platin-Zertifizierung; natürliche Belüftung des Komplexes; natürliche Querlüftung in jeder Wohnung; mehr als 350 Pflanzenarten im grünen Zentrum; Bewässerung mit gesammeltem Regenwasser von Dächern, Terrassen und Fassade; Sonnenblenden aus Mesh-Gewebe verschatten, ohne Luftzirkulation und Tageslichteinfall zu behindern; spezielle Verglasung reduziert Sonneneinstrahlung ins Gebäude; Solarmodule auf dem Dach; Fahrradstellplätze und Ladestationen für Elektrofahrzeuge; direkte Zugänge zu mehreren Metrolinien und Bushaltestellen

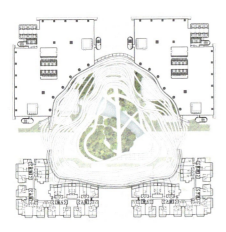

Typical floor plan office and residential
Grundriss Regelgeschoss Büro und Wohnen

Section
Schnitt

ingenhoven architects' largest project to date comprises two office towers, each with 175,000 square metres of floor space, and two residential high-rises accommodating approximately 3,000 inhabitants. Between these structures expands a green centre that is open to the public. Reminiscent of a rainforest, over 350 different tree and plant species grow here. Thanks to its arrangement over several levels, inspired by Asian rice terraces, the surface is 25 percent larger than the original plot of land. The integrated cafés and restaurants, shops and recreational facilities provide meeting places for residents and employees. In addition, the interplay of the buildings' geometry with the green valley generates natural ventilation and, consequently, a pleasant microclimate. The multifunctional, highly-concentrated complex is an interesting prototype for future large-scale projects in the constantly growing megacities located in tropical climates.

Das bisher größte Projekt von ingenhoven architects umfasst zwei Bürotürme mit jeweils 175 000 Quadratmetern Nutzfläche und zwei Wohnhochhäuser für insgesamt etwa 3000 Bewohner. Dazwischen erstreckt sich ein für jedermann zugängliches grünes Zentrum, in dem ähnlich wie in einem Regenwald mehr als 350 verschiedene Baum- und Pflanzenarten wachsen. Dank der Anordnung in mehreren Ebenen, inspiriert von asiatischen Reisterrassen, ist die Fläche 25 Prozent größer als die des ursprünglichen Grundstücks. Die integrierten Cafés und Restaurants, Geschäfte sowie Freizeiteinrichtungen bieten Treffpunkte für die Anwohner und Angestellten. Darüber hinaus erzeugt das Zusammenspiel der Gebäudegeometrie mit dem grünen Tal eine natürliche Ventilation und dadurch ein angenehmes Mikroklima. Der multifunktionale, hochverdichtete Komplex ist ein interessanter Prototyp für künftige Großprojekte in den stetig wachsenden Megacitys mit tropischem Klima.

The International Highrise Award Internationaler Hochhaus Preis **2018**

Nominated Project 2018
Nominiertes Projekt 2018

JAHN
50 WEST
New York NY, USA

Architects Architekten **JAHN**, Chicago IL, USA
Architects of record Lokale Architekten **SLCE Architects**
Client Bauherr **Time Equities Inc**
Structural engineers Tragwerksplanung **DeSimone Consulting Engineers**
MEP Haustechnik **I. M. Robbins, PC**

Height Höhe **240 m**
Storeys Geschosse **64**
Site area Grundstücksfläche **1680 m²**
Ground footprint Bebaute Fläche **897 m²**
Net floor area Nettogeschossfläche **154 120 m²**
Structure Konstruktion **Reinforced concrete** Stahlbeton
Completion Fertigstellung **February** Februar **2018**
Main use Hauptnutzung **Residential** Wohnen

Sustainability
Nachhaltigkeit
Processing LEED Gold Certification; efficient HVAC systems and glazing reduce energy use; low-flow plumbing fixtures reducing potable water use; 12 percent of materials used are recycled; storm detention tanks capable of capturing all the site runoff, preventing it from flooding the municipal sewers; irrigation entirely by captured rainwater
LEED-Gold-Zertifizierung wird angestrebt; effiziente Heizungs-, Lüftungs- und Klimasysteme sowie Verglasung reduzieren Energieverbrauch; wassersparende Armaturen reduzieren Verbrauch; 12 Prozent der genutzten Materialien sind recycelt; Speicherbecken nehmen (auch bei Unwetter) den gesamten Niederschlag des Grundstücks auf, sodass dies nicht die Kanalisation flutet; Bewässerung vollständig mit gesammeltem Regenwasser

Site plan
Lageplan

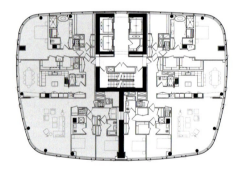

Typical floor plan
Grundriss Regelgeschoss

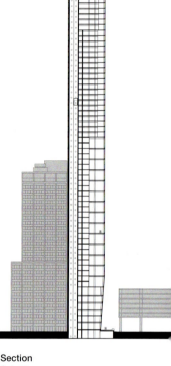

Section
Schnitt

All four corners of the building are rounded off throughout its entire height, thanks to the use of 500 curved glass panels. These grant the apartments, some of which are of two storeys, unobstructed views of the East and Hudson Rivers or even all the way to the Statue of Liberty, undisturbed by window profiles. In this way, the slender, elegant residential tower takes advantage of its prominent location between Ground Zero and the southern tip of Manhattan. The roof terrace, framed by a sharp-cornered, chamfered band of concrete and accessible to all residents of the 191 exclusive apartments, offers additional views.

The tower is tapered at its base to provide space for a newly designed open square. From here, it is connected to the riverbank via the new West Thames Street Pedestrian Bridge and Rector Park.

Über die gesamte Höhe des Hochhauses sind alle vier Gebäudeecken unter Einsatz von 500 gebogenen Glasmodulen abgerundet. Aus den teilweise zweigeschossigen Wohnräumen ermöglichen sie ohne störende Fensterprofile freie Sicht auf East und Hudson River bis hin zur Freiheitsstatue. So nutzt der schlanke, elegante Wohnturm seine exponierte Lage zwischen Ground Zero und der südlichen Spitze Manhattans. Zusätzliche Ausblicke bietet die von einem scharfkantigen, abgeschrägten Betonband gefasste Dachterrasse, die allen Bewohnern der 191 exklusiven Wohnungen zur Verfügung steht.

An seiner Basis verjüngt sich der Turm, um Raum für einen neu gestalteten öffentlichen Platz zu schaffen. Von dort ist er über die neue West Thames Street Pedestrian Bridge und den Rector Park an das Ufer angebunden.

The International Highrise Award Internationaler Hochhaus Preis **2018**

Nominated Project 2018
Nominiertes Projekt 2018

Kohn Pedersen Fox Associates
LOTTE WORLD TOWER
Seoul, South Korea Südkorea

Architects Architekten **Kohn Pedersen Fox Associates, New York NY, USA**
Project architects Projektarchitekten **Terri Cho; Paul Bae; Younhak Jeong**
Architects of record Lokale Architekten **BAUM**
Client Bauherr **Lotte Group**
Structural engineers Tragwerksplanung **Leslie E. Robertson Associates**
MEP Haustechnik **Syska Hennessy Group**

Height Höhe **555 m**
Storeys Geschosse **123**
Site area Grundstücksfläche **87 200 m²**
Net floor area Nettogeschossfläche **307 000 m²**
Structure Konstruktion **Composite** Verbundbauweise
Completion Fertigstellung **March** März **2017**

Main use Hauptnutzung **Mixed use comprising office, residential, hotel, restaurants, healthcare, culture and retail** Mischnutzung aus Büros, Wohnen, Hotel, Restaurants, Gesundheitsversorgung, Kultur und Einzelhandel

Sustainability
Nachhaltigkeit
LEED Gold Certified; building generates up to 14.5 percent of its own energy consumption; geothermal mass system using constant temperature 200 metres below ground level to heat in winter and cool in summer; photovoltaic panels; wind turbines; building envelope reduces solar gains; water harvesting systems
LEED-Gold-Zertifizierung; Gebäude generiert bis zu 14,5 Prozent seines Energieverbrauchs selbst; Erdwärmeanlage nutzt konstante Temperatur in 200 Metern Tiefe zum Heizen im Winter und Kühlen im Sommer; Solarmodule; Windkraftanlagen; Gebäudehülle reduziert Aufheizen durch Sonnenstrahlung; Regenwassernutzungsanlage

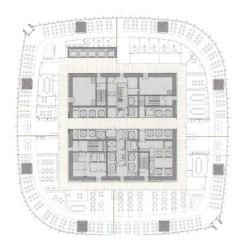

Typical floor plan office
Grundriss Regelgeschoss Büro

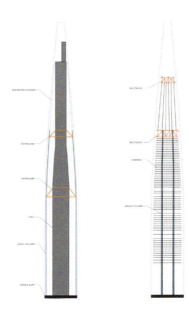

Sections
Schnitte

With the Lotte World Tower and the Ping An Finance Centre (pp. 104–105) – 50 metres higher still – Kohn Pedersen Fox now account for places five and four in the list of the world's highest buildings.

Despite its enormous height and mix of usage, the Lotte World Tower still makes a very elegant impression. This is achieved through its light, porous glass and aluminium façade as well as its upwardly tapering form, inspired by historic ceramics and calligraphy. The lobby, with its clear lines, curved shapes and use of white porcelain and oak as design materials, likewise quotes the traditional techniques of Korean craftsmanship.

Structurally, the square-based tower rests on eight mega-columns, additionally supported by the core, plus outriggers and belt trusses on the middle and upper storeys.

Mit dem Lotte World Tower und dem sogar noch 50 Meter höheren Ping An Finance Centre (S. 104–105) haben Kohn Pedersen Fox zuletzt die Plätze Fünf und Vier der weltweit höchsten Gebäude neu besetzt.

Der Lotte World Tower wirkt dabei trotz seiner enormen Höhe und der vielfältigen Nutzungsmischung sehr elegant. Grund dafür sind die leichte, durchlässige Fassade aus Glas und Aluminium sowie die sich nach oben verjüngende Form, die von historischer Keramik und Kalligraphie inspiriert ist. Die Lobby mit ihren klaren Linien, geschwungenen Formen und den verwendeten Materialien weißes Porzellan und Eichenholz zitiert ebenfalls traditionelle koreanische Handwerkstechniken.

Statisch ruht der Turm mit quadratischer Grundfläche auf acht Mega-Stützen; zusätzlich ausgesteift wird er durch den Kern sowie in den mittleren und oberen Geschossen durch Stützausleger und Fachwerkgürtel.

The International Highrise Award Internationaler Hochhaus Preis 2018

Nominated Project 2018
Nominiertes Projekt 2018

Kohn Pedersen Fox Associates
PING AN FINANCE CENTRE
Shenzhen, China

Architects Architekten **Kohn Pedersen Fox Associates, New York NY, USA**
Project architects Projektarchitekten **Paul Katz; David Malott**
Architects of record Lokale Architekten **China Construction Design International**
Client Bauherr **Ping An Insurance Company**
Structural engineers Tragwerksplanung **Thornton Tomasetti**
MEP Haustechnik **J. Roger Preston Group**

Height Höhe **600 m**
Storeys Geschosse **115**
Site area Grundstücksfläche **18 900 m²**
Net floor area Nettogeschossfläche **382 000 m²**
Structure Konstruktion **Composite** Verbundbauweise
Completion Fertigstellung **January** Januar **2017**
Main use Hauptnutzung **Office and retail** Büros und Einzelhandel

Sustainability
Nachhaltigkeit
LEED Gold Certified; efficient cooling with ice storage system; grey water recycling; rainwater collection for irrigation; conversion of the lifts' braking energy into electricity; energy management system built around the BIM model
LEED-Gold-Zertifizierung; effiziente Kühlung durch Eisspeichersystem; Grauwasser-Recycling; Regenwassersammlung zur Bewässerung; Umwandlung von Bremsenergie der Aufzüge in Strom; Energiemanagement nach BIM

  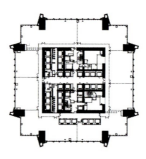

Typical floor plans high / mid / low
Grundrisse Regelgeschosse oben / Mitte / unten

In contrast to the elegant, also super-tall Lotte World Tower (pp. 102–103), the fourth-tallest building in the world flaunts its massive quality, with its eight limestone-clad mega-columns anchoring it firmly to the ground. Providing additional stability are the belt trusses – which also divide the tower visually into sections – the outriggers, and the striking chevron brace systems, which not only increase the stiffness of the construction but also function as lightning conductors. The aerodynamic, sharply tapered shape of the tower, with its inwardly folded corners, reduces wind loads by 40 percent – a significant index in a region threatened by typhoons. While the tower itself contains over 100 storeys of office space for the eponymous insurance company, its base forms a ten-storey terraced shopping centre that opens onto the urban environment.

Im Gegensatz zum eleganten, ebenfalls *supertall* Lotte World Tower (S. 102–103) kokettiert das vierthöchste Gebäude der Welt durchaus mit seiner Masse, indem seine acht Mega-Stützen im Erdgeschoss mit Kalkstein verkleidet schwer auf dem Boden lasten. Für zusätzliche Stabilität sorgen die Fachwerkgürtel, die den Turm auch visuell in Einheiten gliedern, die Stützausleger sowie die markanten Strebepfeiler, die nicht nur die Steifigkeit der Konstruktion erhöhen, sondern darüber hinaus auch als Blitzableiter fungieren. Die aerodynamische, spitz zulaufende Form des Turms mit seinen eingefalteten Ecken reduziert die auftreffenden Windlasten um 40 Prozent – eine wichtige Kennziffer in einer von Taifunen bedrohten Region. Während der Turm selbst mehr als 100 Bürogeschosse für das namensgebende Versicherungsunternehmen beherbergt, öffnet sich der Sockel in Form eines 10-geschossigen, terrassenartig aufgebauten Einkaufszentrums zum Stadtraum.

The International Highrise Award Internationaler Hochhaus Preis **2018**

Nominated Project 2018
Nominiertes Projekt 2018

Meixner Schlüter Wendt Architekten
NEUER HENNINGER TURM
Frankfurt am Main, Germany Deutschland

Architects Architekten Meixner Schlüter Wendt Architekten, Frankfurt am Main
Project architects Projektarchitekten Claudia Meixner; Florian Schlüter; Martin Wendt
Client Bauherr Actris Henninger Turm GmbH & Co. KG
Structural engineers Tragwerksplanung EHS beratende Ingenieure für Bauwesen GmbH
MEP Haustechnik K. Dörflinger GmbH & Co KG; IPB Ing-Büro Peter Berchtold

Height Höhe 140 m
Storeys Geschosse 40
Site area Grundstücksfläche 13 000 m²
Ground footprint Bebaute Fläche 7300 m²
Net floor area Nettogeschossfläche 56 300 m²

Structure Konstruktion Reinforced concrete Stahlbeton
Completion Fertigstellung March März 2018
Main use Hauptnutzung Residential Wohnen

Sustainability
Nachhaltigkeit
Increased noise protection through triple glazing and loggias between living space and exterior; geothermal heat pump; heating and ventilation use heat recovery; natural ventilation; energy-efficient lifts; green roofs on top of pedestal; LED lighting of public and semi-public spaces; electric vehicle charging stations; nesting site for hawks
Erhöhter Schallschutz durch Dreifachverglasung und Loggien zwischen Wohn- und Außenraum; Erdwärmepumpe; Heizung und Lüftung mit Wärmerückgewinnung; natürliche Belüftung; energieeffiziente Aufzüge; Gründächer auf der Sockelbebauung; Beleuchtung der öffentlichen und halböffentlichen Bereiche durch LEDs; Stellplätze mit Stromversorgung für Elektrofahrzeuge; Falkennistplatz

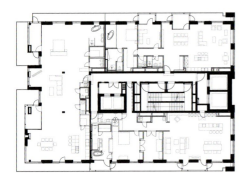

Floor plan level 30
Grundriss 30. Obergeschoss

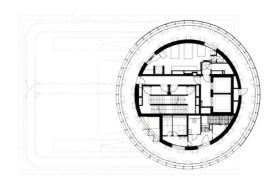

Floor plan level 38
Grundriss 38. Obergeschoss

The unusual appearance of this residential high-rise has historic roots. The site was previously occupied by a striking but eventually redundant grain silo belonging to the Henninger Brewery, the image of which – with its cubic shape topped by a barrel that included a revolving restaurant – was etched into the city's collective memory. The new structure pays homage to this silhouette as an 'emotional monument'; however, due to its function as a residential space (209 apartments), it comprises more volume. While the northern façade, that faces the city centre, recalls the block-like outer appearance of the previous building, on the other sides, balconies and winter gardens in colossal order open to the exterior. The 'barrel' will once again be occupied by a restaurant, added to by exclusive apartments. Surrounding the tower is an open square, defined by a new perimeter development that includes shops, a fitness studio, a restaurant and a multi-storey carpark.

Die ungewöhnliche Erscheinung dieses Wohnhochhauses hat historische Gründe. Zuvor stand an dieser Stelle ein markantes, aber mittlerweile funktionslos gewordenes Getreidesilo der Brauerei Henninger, das sich durch seine kubische Form und das aufgesetzte Fass samt Drehrestaurant in das kollektive Stadtgedächtnis eingebrannt hatte. Der Neubau ist dieser Silhouette als „emotionales Denkmal" nachempfunden, umfasst aber aufgrund der Wohnnutzung (209 Wohnungen) mehr Volumen. Während die der Stadt zugewandte Nordfassade noch an die blockartige Außenwirkung des Vorgängerbaus erinnert, öffnen sich an den anderen Seiten nun Balkone und Wintergärten in Kolossalordnung nach außen. In das „Fass" zieht neben exklusiven Wohnungen auch wieder ein Restaurant ein. Umgeben ist der Turm von einem öffentlichen Platz, definiert durch eine neue Randbebauung, die mehrere Nahversorger, ein Fitnessstudio, eine Gaststätte und ein Parkhaus beherbergt.

The International Highrise Award Internationaler Hochhaus Preis 2018

Nominated Project 2018
Nominiertes Projekt 2018

NBBJ
TENCENT SEAFRONT HEADQUARTERS
Shenzhen, China

Architects Architekten **NBBJ, Los Angeles CA, USA**
Project architect Projektarchitekt **Jonathan Ward**
Architects of record Lokale Architekten **Tongji Architectural Design (Group) Co, Ltd**
Client Bauherr **Tencent Holdings Ltd**
Structural engineers Tragwerksplanung **AECOM**
MEP Haustechnik **WSP Group**

Height Höhe **250 m**
Storeys Geschosse **50**
Site area Grundstücksfläche **18 651 m²**
Ground footprint Bebaute Fläche **7274 m²**
Net floor area Nettogeschossfläche **266 200 m²**
Structure Konstruktion **Composite** Verbundbauweise
Completion Fertigstellung **November 2017**
Main use Hauptnutzung **Office** Büros

Sustainability
Nachhaltigkeit

Energy consumption and carbon emissions reduced by 40 percent over a typical office tower; outdoor gardens on the roofs of the sky bridges; slight rotation of the towers and their offset heights capture prevailing winds while minimizing exposure to direct sunlight; curtain wall incorporates a shading system adapting to the sun's arc; modular pattern additionally shades south façade; bioswales and permeable surfaces help absorb storm-water runoff

Energieverbrauch und CO_2-Emissionen um 40 Prozent geringer als bei typischem Büro-Hochhaus; Dachgärten auf den sky bridges; die leicht versetzte Anordnung und unterschiedliche Höhe der Türme fängt Wind ein und minimiert direkte Sonneneinstrahlung; Vorhangfassade enthält Sonnenschutzsystem, das sich dem Sonnenstand anpasst; modulare Profilierung der Südfassade sorgt für zusätzliche Verschattung; biologische Regenwasserreinigung und -versickerung

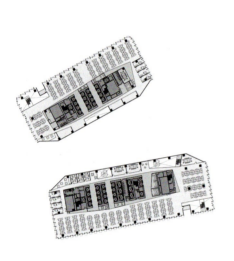

Typical floor plan
Grundriss Regelgeschoss

Diagram average travel distance
Diagramm durchschnittlicher Entfernungen

While until recently technology companies have made their homes on expansive suburban campuses, they are now moving increasingly into city centres. The NBBJ architecture firm has taken this step with Amazon in Seattle – and in Shenzhen, with the Chinese internet giant Tencent. Here, the lively and communicative campus lifestyle was transferred into the dense, vertical structure of two high rise slabs by incorporating three sky bridges that connect the towers to one another like digital links. They not only shorten walking distances but under the key terms of Culture, Knowledge and Health they contribute to the well-being of the company's employees and their internal exchanges. The facilities include community spaces, a library and sports areas such as a running track and a pool.

Nachdem die meisten Technologiekonzerne sich bisher auf weitläufigen, suburbanen Campusanlagen angesiedelt haben, zieht es sie nun vermehrt in die Innenstädte. Das Architekturbüro NBBJ ist diesen Schritt mit Amazon in Seattle gegangen – und in Shenzen mit dem chinesischen Internetriesen Tencent. Hier wurde das lebendige und kommunikative Campusleben in die dichte, vertikale Struktur zweier Hochhausscheiben übertragen, indem drei sky bridges die Türme wie digitale Links miteinander verbinden. Sie verkürzen nicht nur die Wege, sondern tragen unter den Stichworten Kultur, Wissen und Gesundheit auch zum Wohlbefinden der Beschäftigten und zu deren internem Austausch bei. Zur Ausstattung gehören unter anderem Gemeinschaftsräume, eine Bibliothek und Sportanlagen wie eine Laufbahn oder ein Schwimmbad.

The International Highrise Award Internationaler Hochhaus Preis **2018**

Nominated Project 2018
Nominiertes Projekt 2018

Pelli Clarke Pelli Architects
SALESFORCE TOWER
San Francisco CA, USA

Architects Architekten **Pelli Clarke Pelli Architects, New Haven CT, USA**
Project architects Projektarchitekten **César Pelli; Fred W. Clarke**
Architects of record Lokale Architekten **Kendall Heaton Associates**
Clients Bauherren **Boston Properties, Inc; Hines Interests Limited Partnership**
Structural engineers Tragwerksplanung **Magnusson Klemencic Associates**
MEP Haustechnik **WSP Group**

Height Höhe **326 m**
Storeys Geschosse **61**
Site area Grundstücksfläche **5574 m²**
Ground footprint Bebaute Fläche **2323 m²**
Net floor area Nettogeschossfläche **150 000 m²**
Structure Konstruktion **Composite** Verbundbauweise
Completion Fertigstellung **January** Januar **2018**
Main use Hauptnutzung **Office** Büros

Sustainability
Nachhaltigkeit
Low-emissivity glass; horizontal metal fins on the façade act as sunshades; heat-exchanging coils; water recycling systems; fresh air provided by air-handlers underneath the 12-inch raised floors; directly adjacent to intermodal transit station
Isolierglas; metallene Fenstersimse dienen gleichzeitig als Sonnenschutz; Wärmetauscher; Abwasseraufbereitung; Frischluftzufuhr per Lüftungsanlage unter 30 Zentimeter angehobenen Fußböden; unmittelbar angrenzend an intermodalen Verkehrsknotenpunkt

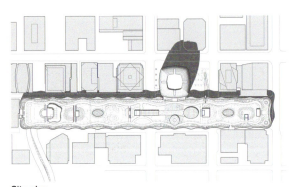

Site plan
Lageplan

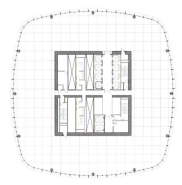

Typical floor plan
Grundriss Regelgeschoss

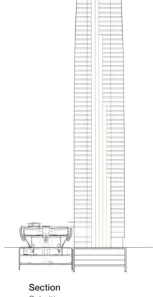

Section
Schnitt

The slender, tapering office tower has the timeless shape of a rounded obelisk, with an all-glass façade outlined by a metal framework. A 60-metre-deep concrete foundation and a solid core of reinforced concrete secure the structure against high winds and earthquakes.

At its top, the building, currently San Francisco's highest, is home to the world's highest-elevation work of public art. At night, an installation by the artist Jim Campbell employs 11,000 LED lights to project a spectacle of images collected throughout the course of the day by cameras located around the city.

The adjacent multi-modal transport hub, the Transbay Transit Center, was also designed by Pelli Clarke Pelli Architects. Its extensive roof garden directly connects to the fourth-storey level of the Salesforce Tower.

Insgesamt hat der schmale, sich verjüngende Büroturm die zeitlose Gestalt eines abgerundeten Obelisken mit vollverglaster Fassade, konturiert durch eine Metallstruktur. Ein 60 Meter tiefes Betonfundament und ein massiver Kern aus Stahlbeton sichern den Turm gegen starke Winde und Erdbeben ab.

An seiner Spitze verfügt das höchste Gebäude San Franciscos über das weltweit höchstgelegene Kunstwerk im öffentlichen Raum. Eine Installation des Künstlers Jim Campell zeigt nachts unter Einsatz von 11 000 LEDs Bilder, die verschiedene Kameras in der Stadt tagsüber zu diesem Zweck aufgenommen haben.

Der angrenzende multimodale Verkehrsknotenpunkt Transbay Transit Center wurde ebenfalls von Pelli Clarke Pelli Architects entworfen. Mit dessen großflächigem Dachgarten ist der Salesforce Tower im vierten Stock direkt verbunden.

The International Highrise Award Internationaler Hochhaus Preis 2018

Nominated Project 2018
Nominiertes Projekt 2018

Renzo Piano Building Workshop
TRIBUNAL DE PARIS
Paris, France Frankreich

Architects Architekten **Renzo Piano Building Workshop, Paris**
Project architect Projektarchitekt **Bernhard Plattner**
Clients Bauherren **Bouygues Bâtiment Ile-de-France; Agence Arélia**
Structural engineers Tragwerksplanung **SETEC TPI**
MEP Haustechnik **SETEC Bâtiment; Berim**

Height Höhe **160 m**
Storeys Geschosse **38**
Site area Grundstücksfläche **17 500 m²**
Ground footprint Bebaute Fläche **17 500 m²**
Net floor area Nettogeschossfläche **110 000 m²**
Structure Konstruktion **Composite** Verbundbauweise
Completion Fertigstellung **August 2017**
Main use Hauptnutzung **Courthouse** Gerichtsgebäude

Sustainability
Nachhaltigkeit
HQE (high environmental quality) and BBC (low energy consumption) Certification; natural ventilation; three planted terraces; vertical and horizontal photovoltaic panels; energy performance respects the goals of the Paris Climate Plan and the French Thermal Regulation (RT2012) requirements; energy consumption limited to half compared to most recent office towers in the La Défense business district of Paris
Zertifizierung nach HQE (hohe ökologische Qualität) und BBC (geringer Energieverbrauch); natürliche Belüftung; drei bepflanzte Terrassen; vertikale und horizontale Solarmodule; Energieeffizienz folgt den Zielen des Pariser Klimaabkommens und den Vorgaben der französischen Wärmeverordnung (RT2012); Energieverbrauch reduziert auf die Hälfte verglichen mit den meisten kürzlich gebauten Bürohochhäusern im Pariser Geschäftsviertel La Défense

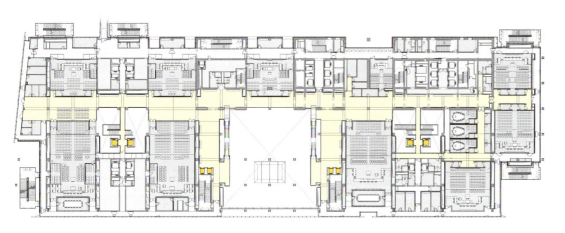

Floor plan level 2
Grundriss 2. Obergeschoss

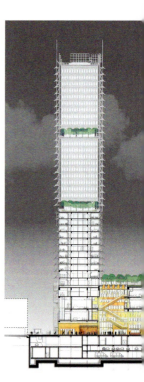

Section
Schnitt

France's largest judicial institution, in terms of cases tried, is the Tribunale de Grande Instance. Its location in the historic Palais de Justice having grown too small, it now occupies a new building containing 90 courtrooms and numerous office spaces. This is located directly on the Boulevard Périphérique ring road, near the border to the suburb of Clichy and far removed from the business district of La Défense. The fully glazed high-rise thus represents a flagship project of the government's 'Grand Paris' programme, which aims to link the urban core more closely with its surrounding area. The stepped arrangement of the three cuboids set on a broad pedestal creates three large roof gardens. The heart of the complex is the 28-metre-high, light-suffused lobby with its slender steel columns. It symbolises the transparency of the judicial decisions that are delivered here.

Weil der bisherige Sitz im innerstädtischen historischen Palais de Justice zu klein für das nach Fällen größte französische Gericht, das Tribunal de Grande Instance, geworden war, wurde ein neuer Hauptsitz mit 90 Gerichtssälen und zahlreichen Büros errichtet. Er liegt direkt an der Ringautobahn nahe der Grenze zur Vorstadt Clichy, weit entfernt vom Geschäftsviertel La Défense. Das vollverglaste Hochhaus ist damit ein Leuchtturm-Projekt des politischen Programms „Grand Paris", das die Kernstadt stärker mit ihrem Umland vernetzen soll. Durch die abgetreppte Stapelung der drei Quader auf einem breiten Sockel ergeben sich drei große Dachgärten. Herzstück des Komplexes ist die 28 Meter hohe, lichtdurchflutete Eingangshalle mit ihren schmalen Stahlstützen. Sie symbolisiert die Transparenz der hier getroffenen gerichtlichen Entscheidungen.

The International Highrise Award Internationaler Hochhaus Preis 2018

Nominated Project 2018
Nominiertes Projekt 2018

SCDA Architects
ECHELON
Singapore Singapur

Architects Architekten **SCDA Architects, Singapore** Singapur
Project architect Projektarchitekt **Soo K. Chan**
Architects of record Lokale Architekten **NIL**
Client Bauherr **City Developments Limited (CDL)**
Structural engineers Tragwerksplanung **KTP**
MEP Haustechnik **Squire Mech**

Height Höhe **163 m**
Storeys Geschosse **43**
Site area Grundstücksfläche **9950 m²**
Gross floor area Bruttogeschossfläche **49 525 m²**

Structure Konstruktion **Reinforced concrete frame** Stahlbetonrahmenkonstruktion
Completion Fertigstellung **November 2016**
Main use Hauptnutzung **Residential** Wohnen

Sustainability
Nachhaltigkeit
BCA Green Mark Platinum Award; large environmental entrance area; landscaped sky lounges; north-south orientation of larger units to maximize natural light and ventilation; energy efficient T5 and LED lighting; ductless fans for basement ventilation; cool paint on west and east façades
BCA-Green-Mark-Platinum-Award; großer landschaftlich gestalteter Eingangsbereich; begrünte *sky lounges;* Nord-Süd-Ausrichtung der größeren Wohnungen für natürliche Belüftung und Tageslicht; energieeffiziente T5- und LED-Beleuchtung; Filterabzug für Belüftung der Untergeschosse; Sonne reflektierender, kühlender Anstrich der West- und Ostfassade

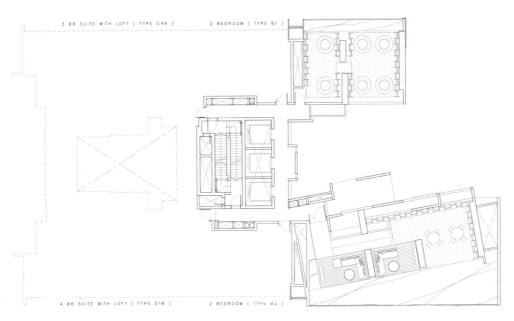

Floor plan levels 13 and 28
Grundriss 13. und 28. Obergeschoss

In order to optically reduce the building's overall volume, Echelon consists of two identical towers that face opposite sides of the property. They are divided horizontally by sky lounges which extend over two to four storeys, as diagonal cut-outs that break up the uniform curtain wall façade.

Echelon comprises a total of over 500 apartments of various types, stacked in a modular construction design. Every size – from one- or two-room apartments to four-bedroom flats with two-storey living areas – is represented on each level. The larger apartments, with three or four bedrooms, face north and south to counteract the effects of Singapore's tropical climate through cross-ventilation. Balconies attached to the living and dining areas are standard in all apartments.

Um das Gesamtvolumen optisch zu reduzieren, besteht Echelon aus zwei identischen Türmen, die sich zu entgegengesetzten Seiten des Grundstücks wenden. Horizontal gegliedert werden sie von *sky lounges,* die sich über zwei bis vier Geschosse erstrecken und als schräge Einschübe die einheitliche Vorhangfassade aufbrechen.

In modularer Bauweise gestapelt enthält Echelon insgesamt mehr als 500 Wohnungen unterschiedlicher Typen. Dabei sind auf jeder Etage alle Größen von Ein- oder Zweizimmerwohnungen bis hin zu Apartments mit vier Schlafzimmern und doppelgeschossigen Wohnbereichen vertreten. Die größeren Wohnungen ab drei Schlafzimmern sind nach Norden und Süden ausgerichtet, um dem tropischen Klima Singapurs durch Querlüftung zu begegnen. Ein Balkon, der sich an den Wohn- und Essbereich anschließt, ist Standard in allen Wohnungen.

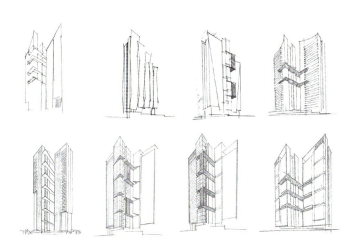

The International Highrise Award Internationaler Hochhaus Preis 2018

Nominated Project 2018
Nominiertes Projekt 2018

SHoP Architects
461 DEAN STREET
New York NY, USA

Architects Architekten **SHoP Architects, New York**
Client Bauherr **Forest City Ratner Companies**
Structural engineers Tragwerksplanung **Arup**
MEP Haustechnik **Arup**

Height Höhe **109 m**
Storeys Geschosse **32**
Site area Grundstücksfläche **1056 m²**
Ground footprint Bebaute Fläche **896 m²**
Net floor area Nettogeschossfläche **32 165 m²**
Structure Konstruktion **Steel** Stahl
Completion Fertigstellung **December** Dezember **2017**
Main use Hauptnutzung **Residential** Wohnen

Sustainability
Nachhaltigkeit
LEED Silver Certified; modular construction reduces embodied energy; roughly one third the weight of a concrete structure of similar size and configuration
LEED-Silber-Zertifizierung; modulare Bauweise reduziert graue Energie; ungefähr ein Drittel des Gewichts einer vergleichbaren Betonkonstruktion

Typical floor plan
Grundriss Regelgeschoss

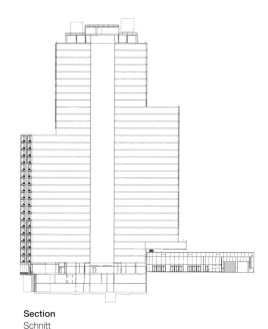

Section
Schnitt

The tallest modular building in the world is made up of 930 prefabricated units, which were delivered by truck and stacked on site. This prototype demonstrates that a modular building can meet the same demands as a standard high-rise, for example a variety of apartment floor plans. The short building phase envisaged for the pilot project could not be realised, due to technical start-up difficulties. Affordable living space was created nonetheless: of the 363 apartment units, half are intended for low and middle-income residents. A total of 84,000 applications were submitted for these 181 subsidised units.

Along with the multifunctional Barclays Center arena, likewise designed by SHoP Architects, 461 Dean Street is the first part of the new Pacific Park development to be completed. This will comprise 6,500 apartments, one third of them at affordable rents.

Das höchste modulare Gebäude der Welt besteht aus 930 vorgefertigten Einheiten, die per LKW angeliefert und vor Ort gestapelt wurden. Der Prototyp zeigt, dass ein modulares Gebäude durchaus die gleichen Anforderungen wie ein herkömmliches Hochhaus erfüllen kann, zum Beispiel unterschiedliche Wohnungsgrundrisse. Die theoretisch kurze Bauzeit konnte wegen technischer Startschwierigkeiten nicht eingehalten werden. Erschwinglicher Wohnraum ist dennoch entstanden: Die Hälfte der 363 Wohnungen ist Niedrig- und Mittelverdienenden zugedacht. Für diese 181 geförderten Einheiten gab es 84 000 Bewerbungen.

461 Dean Street ist zusammen mit der Multifunktionsarena Barclays Center, ebenfalls gestaltet von SHoP Architects, der erste fertiggestellte Teil des neuen Quartiers Pacific Park, das einmal 6500 Wohnungen umfassen soll – ein Drittel davon zu sozialverträglichen Mieten.

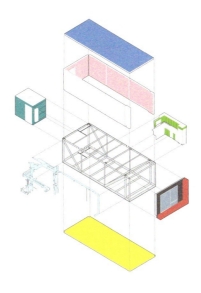

The International Highrise Award Internationaler Hochhaus Preis 2018

Nominated Project 2018
Nominiertes Projekt 2018

SHoP Architects
AMERICAN COPPER BUILDINGS
New York NY, USA

Architects Architekten **SHoP Architects, New York**
Client Bauherr **JDS Development Group**
Structural engineers Tragwerksplanung **WSP Cantor Seinuk**
MEP Haustechnik **Buro Happold**

Height Höhe **156 m; 134 m**
Storeys Geschosse **48; 41**
Site area Grundstücksfläche **4198 m²**
Ground footprint Bebaute Fläche **1746 m²**
Net floor area Nettogeschossfläche **76 645 m²**
Structure Konstruktion **Reinforced concrete** Stahlbeton
Completion Fertigstellung **April 2018**
Main use Hauptnutzung **Residential** Wohnen

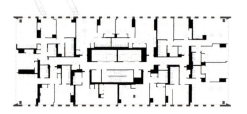

Floor plan level 34
Grundriss 34. Obergeschoss

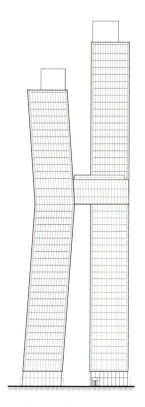

East elevation
Ostansicht

The American Copper Buildings take their name from the copper cladding on their longitudinal sides; the use of the material was inspired by the Statue of Liberty. Like that monument, the Copper Buildings will lose their reddish-brown colouring over time and take on a mint-green patina.

In response to local building regulations, both towers bend inward in the middle. At a height of over 90 metres, where they come closest to one another, they are linked by a 30-metre-long sky bridge. The bridge houses part of the more than 5,000 square metres of communal space available to the residents of the 761 rental properties – which includes a swimming pool, whirlpool and bar. Thanks to the recent creation of a public park on the riverbank, this site of a former power plant on the East River has increased in attraction for passers-by, too.

Namensgebend für die American Copper Buildings ist die Kupferverkleidung ihrer Längsseiten, die von der Freiheitsstatue inspiriert ist. Ebenso wie diese werden auch die Copper Buildings mit der Zeit ihre rotbräunliche Farbe verlieren und eine mintgrüne Patina ansetzen.

Beide Türme knicken als Reaktion auf örtliche Bauregularien jeweils mittig ein. In über 90 Metern Höhe, wo sie sich am nächsten sind, verbindet sie eine 3-stöckige, 30 Meter lange *sky bridge*. Diese beherbergt einen Teil der mehr als 5000 Quadratmeter umfassenden Gemeinschaftsflächen für die Bewohner der 761 Mietwohnungen, darunter Schwimmbecken, Whirlpool und Bar. Aber auch für Passanten wird der ehemalige Standort eines Kraftwerks am East River durch den neu angelegten öffentlichen Park am Ufer aufgewertet.

The International Highrise Award Internationaler Hochhaus Preis 2018

Nominated Project 2018
Nominiertes Projekt 2018

SimpsonHaugh
DOLLAR BAY
London, UK Großbritannien

Architects Architekten **SimpsonHaugh, London**
Project architects Projektarchitekten **Christian Male; Barbara Clarenz**
Client Bauherr **Mount Anvil**
Structural engineers Tragwerksplanung **WSP Group**
MEP Haustechnik **WSP Group**

Height Höhe **109 m**
Storeys Geschosse **31**
Site area Grundstücksfläche **3182 m²**
Ground footprint Bebaute Fläche **368 m²**
Net floor area Nettogeschossfläche **11 543 m²**
Structure Konstruktion **Composite** Verbundbauweise
Completion Fertigstellung **April 2017**
Main use Hauptnutzung **Residential** Wohnen

Sustainability
Nachhaltigkeit
Dock-water cooling solution; rainwater harvesting for landscape irrigation; green roof; roof solar PV cells; winter gardens work as thermal buffers; private gardens; natural light and ventilation in corridors and lift lobbies; adjustable louvres and openable windows; façade elements of fritted glass or with gold mesh interlayers reduce solar heat gain
Kühlung mit Dock-Wasser; Regenwassersammlung zur Bewässerung; Solarmodule auf dem begrünten Dach; vorgelagerte Wintergärten als thermischer Puffer; private Gärten; natürlich beleuchtete und belüftete Flure und Aufzugsvorräume; verstellbare Lüftungsschlitze und zu öffnende Fenster; Fassadenelemente aus Glasfritten oder mit goldener Mesh-Gewebeschicht reduzieren ein Aufheizen durch Sonne

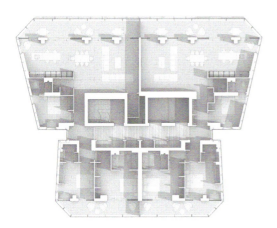

Floor plan level 27
Grundriss 27. Obergeschoss

Façade detail windows
Fassadendetail Fenster

Two crystalline forms connected by a joint circulation core make up Dollar Bay, with room on every level for up to five spacious apartments. On the western and eastern façades, a ceiling-high winter garden extends along the entire width of each flat, expanding the living space outward while simultaneously providing natural ventilation.

The horizontally folded western façade, which faces Canary Wharf, reflects both the water and the sky, evoking the image of a waterfall, while the eastern façade offers unobstructed views to the Thames. The tower tapers at its base to accommodate the renovated waterfront promenade on the South Dock, which features public green space, seating elements and a café.

The use of prefabricated building components made it possible to complete the structure six months ahead of schedule.

Zwei kristalline Formen verbunden durch den gemeinsamen Erschließungskern bilden Dollar Bay und bieten auf jeder Etage Platz für bis zu fünf großzügige Wohnungen. Diesen sind entlang der West- und Ostfassade über die gesamte Breite raumhohe Wintergärten vorgelagert, die den Wohnraum nach außen erweitern und zugleich natürlich belüften.

Die horizontal gefaltete Westfassade mit Ausblick auf Canary Wharf reflektiert sowohl das Wasser als auch den Himmel und erinnert dabei an einen Wasserfall. Zur anderen Seite bietet die Ostfassade freie Sicht auf die Themse. Am Boden verjüngt sich der Turm zugunsten der erneuerten Uferpromenade des South Dock mit öffentlichem Grünraum, Sitzgelegenheiten und einem Café.

Die Verwendung vorgefertigter Bauteile ermöglichte es, das Gebäude ein halbes Jahr früher als ursprünglich geplant fertigzustellen.

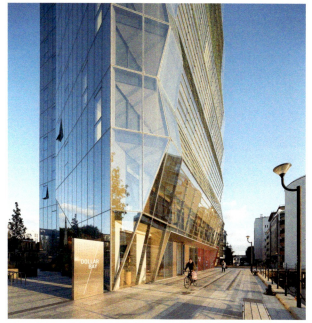

The International Highrise Award Internationaler Hochhaus Preis **2018** 121

Nominated Project 2018
Nominiertes Projekt 2018

Skidmore, Owings & Merrill LLP
POLY INTERNATIONAL PLAZA
Beijing Peking, China

Architects Architekten **Skidmore, Owings & Merrill LLP**, San Francisco CA, USA
Project architect Projektarchitekt **Leo Chow**
Architects of record Lokale Architekten **Zhubo Architectural & Engineering Design Co Ltd**
Client Bauherr **China Poly Real Estate Company Ltd**
Structural engineers Tragwerksplanung **Zhubo Architectural & Engineering Design Co Ltd**
MEP Haustechnik **WSP Flack & Kurtz**

Height Höhe **161 m**
Storeys Geschosse **31**
Ground footprint Bebaute Fläche **2100 m²**
Gross floor area Bruttogeschossfläche **61 200 m²**
Structure Konstruktion **Composite** Verbundbauweise
Completion Fertigstellung **July** Juli **2016**
Main use Hauptnutzung **Office** Büros

Sustainability
Nachhaltigkeit
Pursuing LEED Gold Certification; interstitial façade space stores heat in winter, vents in summer and provides good quality air on days of heavy pollution; water saving fixtures; greywater recycling of all water used for flushing (part of district-wide municipal system); water-side economizers pre-cool water being used by each chiller; heat recovery utilized for air handling units
Strebt LEED-Gold-Zertifizierung an; Fassaden-Zwischenraum speichert Wärme im Winter, lüftet im Sommer und versorgt mit sauberer Luft an Tagen mit hoher Luftverschmutzung; wassersparende Armaturen; gesamtes Abwasser der Toilettenspülung wird als Grauwasser aufbereitet (Teil eines bezirksweiten kommunalen Systems); Economiser am Ufer kühlen Wasser für Kühlanlagen vor; Abwärmenutzung zum Betrieb von Klimaanlagen

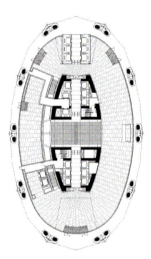

Ground floor plan
Grundriss Erdgeschoss

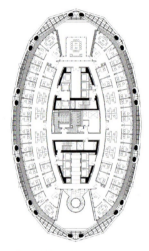

Typical floor plan low-rise
Grundriss Regelgeschoss unten

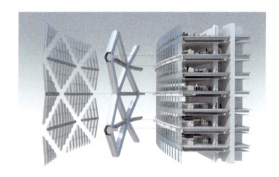

Exploded view façade
Explosionszeichnung Fassade

The three towers of Poly International Plaza are prominently located midway between the Beijing Capital Airport and the Forbidden City. With their elliptical footprint, the towers stand out from the static pattern of the surrounding developments while allowing the adjacent park areas to flow seamlessly into the site.

The main tower's supporting exoskeleton lends the complex its identity; the folded façade was inspired by traditional Chinese lanterns and allows the office spaces to be column-free. These are enclosed in a second, glazed, interior envelope, creating a thermal layer in the space in between, which mediates between Beijing's extreme climate and the work spaces. At the narrow ends of the building, the interstice expands into two 29-storey, nearly building-height atria, which do not only light the floor levels but also permit visual contact with the surrounding storeys.

Exponiert an der Verbindung zwischen dem Flughafen Peking und der Verbotenen Stadt gelegen stehen die drei Türme des Poly International Plaza. Durch ihre elliptischen Grundflächen heben sie sich vom starren Raster der umliegenden Bebauung ab und ermöglichen zugleich eine Fortführung der angrenzenden Parkflächen auf dem Gelände.

Identitätsstiftend ist das tragende Exoskelett des Hauptturms, dessen Faltung von traditionellen chinesischen Lampions inspiriert ist und stützenfreie Büros ermöglicht. Diese werden von einer Innenverglasung umschlossen, sodass im Zwischenraum eine thermische Schicht entsteht. Sie vermittelt zwischen dem extremen Klima Pekings und den Arbeitsräumen. An den schmalen Enden des Gebäudes erweitert sich der Zwischenraum zu zwei 29-stöckigen, beinahe gebäudehohen Atrien, die die Etagen nicht nur beleuchten, sondern auch Blickbeziehungen mit den umliegenden Stockwerken ermöglichen.

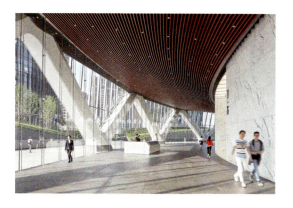

The International Highrise Award Internationaler Hochhaus Preis 2018

Nominated Project 2018
Nominiertes Projekt 2018

Skidmore, Owings & Merrill LLP;
Squire & Partners
THE LEXICON
London, UK Großbritannien

Architects Architekten **Skidmore, Owings & Merrill LLP, London; Squire & Partners, London**
Client Bauherr **Mount Anvil**
Structural engineers Tragwerksplanung **WSP Group**
MEP Haustechnik **Hoare Lea**

Height Höhe **120 m**
Storeys Geschosse **36**
Site area Grundstücksfläche **3945 m²**
Ground footprint Bebaute Fläche **2060 m²**
Net floor area Nettogeschossfläche **18 739 m²**
Structure Konstruktion **Reinforced concrete** Stahlbeton
Completion Fertigstellung **January** Januar **2017**
Main use Hauptnutzung **Residential** Wohnen

Sustainability
Nachhaltigkeit
Interstitial blinds and inset cast-glass channels reduce solar gain; ground-source heat pump powers cooling system of each home; twin-wall ventilated façade insulates against cold and heat; maximizing waste reduction and recycling by prefabrication of façade elements; smart home system with smartphone app
Integrierte Jalousien und eingelassene Gussglas-Kanäle reduzieren solares Aufheizen der Fassade; Wärmepumpe betreibt Klimaanlage jeder Wohnung; belüftete Doppelfassade isoliert gegen Kälte und Hitze; Abfallverringerung und Recycling durch Vorfabrikation der Fassadenelemente; Smart-Home-System mit Smartphone-App

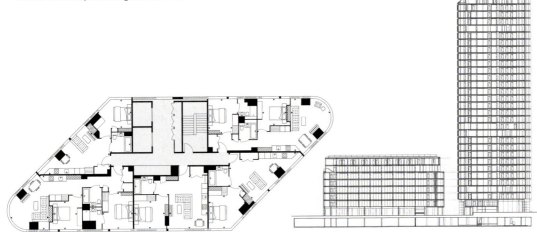

Typical floor plan levels 2–7
Grundriss Regelgeschosse 2–7

Section
Schnitt

In the context of London's continuing skyscraper boom, the elegant Lexicon, situated on the banks of the City Road Basin – together with the neighbouring, somewhat lower Canaletto by UNStudio – symbolises the development of the borough of Islington, to the north of London's financial district.

Lexicon consists of a tower with a slender, diamond-shaped ground plan, along with two accompanying multi-storey buildings which combine to enclose an elongated square. In total, the complex offers space for 300 apartments, about 100 of which are subsidised.

The upper storeys provide exclusive views of London due to the fully glazed curtain wall façade and the building's rounded corners, but especially thanks to the terraces incised into the diagonal roof. At ground level, a restaurant and shops bring life to the public space between the individual buildings and the water's edge.

Im Kontext des anhaltenden Londoner Hochhausbooms symbolisiert das elegante Lexicon am Ufer des City Road Basin gemeinsam mit dem benachbarten, niedrigeren Canaletto von UNStudio die Entwicklung des Stadtteils Islington nördlich des Finanzbezirks der Stadt.

The Lexicon besteht aus einem Turm mit schlankem, rautenförmigem Grundriss sowie zwei dazugehörigen Geschossbauten, die gemeinsam einen länglichen Platz umschließen. Insgesamt bietet der Komplex Platz für 300 Wohnungen, darunter etwa 100 geförderte.

Aus den oberen Stockwerken bieten sich durch die vollverglaste Vorhangfassade und die abgerundeten Gebäudeecken, besonders aber von den in das schräge Dach eingeschnittenen Terrassen exklusive Aussichten auf die Stadt. Am Boden beleben ein Restaurant sowie mehrere Geschäfte den öffentlichen Raum zwischen den einzelnen Gebäuden sowie hin zum Wasser.

The International Highrise Award Internationaler Hochhaus Preis 2018

Nominated Project 2018
Nominiertes Projekt 2018

UNStudio
RAFFLES CITY
Hangzhou, China

Architects Architekten **UNStudio, Amsterdam, Netherlands** Niederlande
Project architects Projektarchitekten **Ben van Berkel; Hannes Pfau; Astrid Piber**
Architects of record Lokale Architekten **China United Engineering Corporation**
Client Bauherr **CapitaLand China**
Structural engineers Tragwerksplanung **Arup**
MEP Haustechnik **SAIYO; Arup**

Height Höhe **250 m**
Storeys Geschosse **60**
Site area Grundstücksfläche **40 355 m²**
Ground footprint Bebaute Fläche **19 128 m²**
Net floor area Nettogeschossfläche **196 977 m²**
Structure Konstruktion **Composite** Verbundbauweise
Completion Fertigstellung **June** Juni **2017**
Main use Hauptnutzung **Mixed use comprising offices, hotel, residential and retail** Mischnutzung aus Büros, Hotel, Wohnen und Einzelhandel

Sustainability
Nachhaltigkeit
LEED Gold Certification; first retail mall in China to use natural ventilation on a large scale; east-west orientation of the towers minimizes overshadowing while maximizing daylight; outer layer of split, vertical solar shading fins; solar energy gain; direct underground connection to the metro
LEED-Gold-Zertifizierung; erstes Shoppingcenter Chinas mit natürlicher Belüftung in diesem Ausmaß; Ost-West-Ausrichtung der Türme verhindert übermäßige Verschattung bei gleichzeitig maximalem Tageslichteinfall; außen liegender Sonnenschutz durch zweigeteilte, vertikale Sonnenblenden; Solareinträge; direkter unterirdischer Zugang zur Metro

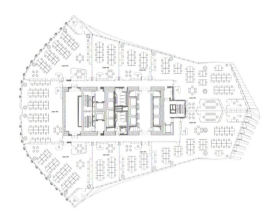

Office floor plan level 11
Büro-Grundriss 11. Obergeschoss

Hotel floor plan level 28
Hotel-Grundriss 28. Obergeschoss

Since the 1980s, the shopping malls of the Singapore-based operator Raffles City have pursued the concept of a 'city within a city'. In keeping with this, the Hangzhou complex also includes a direct underground connection to the metro as well as numerous office spaces, hotel rooms and residential apartments in the two towers above the mall housed in the pedestal. Evoking the movement of the nearby Qiantang River, the flowing shapes of the towers lend the complex a local reference. The elongated concrete support columns follow the same movement, as do the shading panels on the sides that face the sun. The podium is clad in aluminium tiles, reflecting the pulsating life of the surrounding environment, which is active around the clock. Skylights and light shafts fill the mall with daylight and provide visual connections to the towers.

Seit den 1980er-Jahren verfolgt der Shopping Mall-Betreiber Raffles City aus Singapur mit seinen Gebäuden das Konzept der „Stadt in der Stadt". So enthält auch der Standort in Hangzhou einen direkten, unterirdischen Zugang zur Metro und in den beiden Türmen über der Mall im Sockel eine Vielzahl von Büros, Hotelzimmern und Wohnungen. Einen lokalen Bezug schaffen die fließenden Formen der Türme, die auf den Qiantang-Fluss in unmittelbarer Nähe verweisen. Die langgestreckten, tragenden Betonsäulen folgen dieser Bewegung, ebenso wie die schattenspendenden Blenden auf den Sonnenseiten. Der Sockel ist mit Aluminiumkacheln verkleidet, die das pulsierende Leben an diesem rund um die Uhr frequentierten Ort spiegeln. Dachfenster und Lichtschächte beleuchten die Mall mit Tageslicht und stellen Blickbeziehungen zu den Türmen her.

The International Highrise Award Internationaler Hochhaus Preis 2018

Nominated Project 2018
Nominiertes Projekt 2018

UNStudio
THE SCOTTS TOWER
Singapore Singapur

Architects Architekten **UNStudio, Amsterdam, Netherlands** Niederlande
Project architects Projektarchitekten **Ben van Berkel; Astrid Piber**
Architects of record Lokale Architekten **ONG&ONG**
Client Bauherr **Far East Organization**
Structural engineers Tragwerksplanung **KTP Consultants**
MEP Haustechnik **United Project Consultants**

Height Höhe **153 m**
Storeys Geschosse **31**
Site area Grundstücksfläche **6100 m²**
Ground footprint Bebaute Fläche **1075 m²**
Net floor area Nettogeschossfläche **18 500 m²**
Structure Konstruktion **Reinforced concrete** Stahlbeton
Completion Fertigstellung **September 2017**
Main use Hauptnutzung **Residential** Wohnen

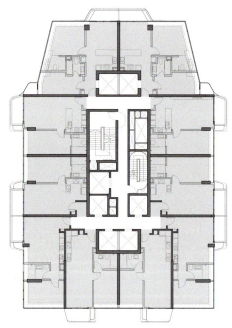

Typical floor plan
Grundriss Regelgeschoss

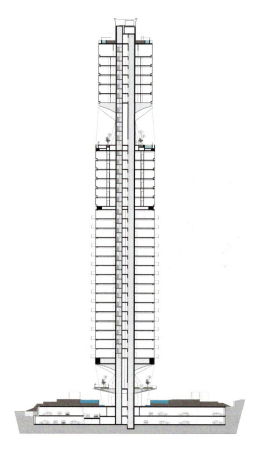

Section
Schnitt

The Scotts Tower is made up of four differently-sized units – dubbed 'neighbourhoods' by the UNStudio architects – which are stacked on top of one another to form a kind of vertical residential district. The size of the apartments increases from one and two-room flats in the lower section to three-room apartments in the middle and four-room penthouses at the tip. In addition to the private balconies, the building's mass is hollowed out in two different locations. Available to all residents, these semi-outdoor spaces are open on all sides of the tower, like large stages facing the city. They comprise gardens and various pools as well as event spaces. The sky lobby above the ground level adds further height to an already existing garden in the entrance area; the sky garden in the upper third of the tower also serves as an observation deck. The roof gardens on the top storey are reserved for penthouse residents.

Aus vier aufeinandergestapelten, unterschiedlich großen Einheiten, die die Architekten von UNStudio als „Nachbarschaften" bezeichnen, bildet der Scotts Tower eine Art vertikales Wohngebiet. Dabei wachsen die Wohnungsgrößen von Ein- und Zweizimmerwohnungen im unteren Bereich über Dreizimmerapartments in der Mitte bis hin zu Vierzimmerpenthouses an der Spitze. Zusätzlich zu den privaten Balkonen ist an zwei Stellen das Volumen des Baukörpers ausgehöhlt. Diese Freiräume für alle Bewohner öffnen sich an jeder Seite des Turms wie große Bühnen zur Stadt. Sie bieten Gärten, verschiedene Pools sowie Platz für Veranstaltungen. Die untere, sogenannte *sky lobby* erweitert einen bereits existierenden Garten im Eingangsbereich in die Höhe, der *sky garden* im oberen Drittel dient gleichzeitig als Aussichtsplattform. Die Dachgärten auf dem obersten Stockwerk sind den Bewohnern der Penthouses vorbehalten.

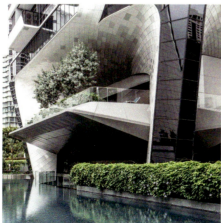

The International Highrise Award Internationaler Hochhaus Preis **2018**

Nominated Project 2018
Nominiertes Projekt 2018

WOHA
HUAKU SKY GARDEN
Taipei Taipeh, Taiwan

Architects Architekten **WOHA, Singapore** Singapur
Project architects Projektarchitekten **Wong Mun Summ; Pearl Chee**
Architects of record Lokale Architekten **C. C. Jen Architects & Associates**
Client Bauherr **Huaku Development Co, Ltd**
Structural engineers Tragwerksplanung **New Structure Group**
MEP Haustechnik **Heng Kai Engineering Consultants Inc**

Height Höhe **153 m**
Storeys Geschosse **38**
Site area Grundstücksfläche **5717 m²**
Ground footprint Bebaute Fläche **1881 m²**
Net floor area Nettogeschossfläche **43 000 m²**
Structure Konstruktion **Composite** Verbundbauweise
Completion Fertigstellung **April 2017**
Main use Hauptnutzung **Residential** Wohnen

Sustainability
Nachhaltigkeit

Double-volume sky garden for each apartment; ornamental screens act as sunshades; dual frontage of each apartment enables natural cross-ventilation; gardens and green walls at street level
Sky garden doppelter Höhe für jede Wohnung; Fassadenverzierungen fungieren als Sonnenschutz; Ausrichtung zu zwei Seiten ermöglicht Querlüftung in jeder Wohnung; Gärten und begrünte Wände auf Straßenniveau

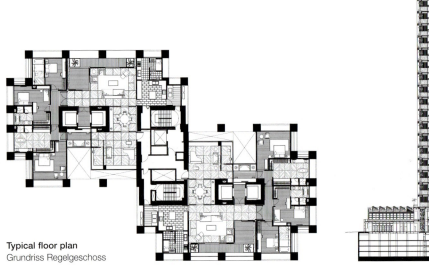

Typical floor plan
Grundriss Regelgeschoss

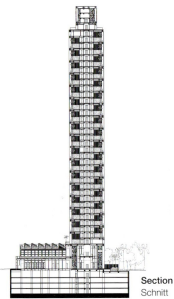

Section
Schnitt

As the only high-rise in the area, Huaku Sky Garden towers up from among the sea of surrounding housing blocks like a giant room screen. Its dominant external columns stabilise the building against earthquakes and typhoons. At the same time, they allow for column-free floor plans in the interior. The delicate metal screen continues this façade structure in the form of ornaments. Each of the single-storey apartments benefits from the interlocking arrangement of the levels through the creation of a double-height sky garden as well as orientation to both sides of the building, providing views of the city and the mountains. In addition, the roof garden is open to residents of every storey.

The fact that the building contractor increased the budget in the course of this project is a rarity in a region of otherwise highly cost-conscious markets. As a result, the interior design was executed using especially high-quality and durable materials.

Wie ein gigantischer Paravent ragt Huaku Sky Garden als einziges Hochhaus aus dem Meer der umliegenden Häuserblocks empor. Dabei verleihen die dominanten, außen liegenden Stützen dem Gebäude Stabilität gegen Erdbeben und Taifune. Zudem ermöglichen sie freie Grundrisse im Inneren. Das filigrane Metallgitter setzt diese Fassadenstruktur als Ornament fort. Durch die ineinander verzahnte Anordnung der Geschosse profitiert jede der eingeschossigen Wohnungen von einem eigenen *sky garden* doppelter Höhe sowie einer Ausrichtung zu zwei Seiten mit Stadt- und Bergblick. Außerdem steht die Dachterrasse den Bewohnern aller Etagen offen.

Eine taiwanische Besonderheit in einer Region ansonsten sehr kostenbewusster Märkte ist der Umstand, dass der Bauherr im Laufe des Projektes das Budget erhöhte. Der Innenausbau wurde daher mit besonders hochwertigen und langlebigen Materialien ausgeführt.

The International Highrise Award Internationaler Hochhaus Preis **2018**

Nominated Project 2018
Nominiertes Projekt 2018

Zaha Hadid Architects
GENERALI TOWER
Milan Mailand, Italy Italien

Architects Architekten Zaha Hadid Architects, London, UK Großbritannien
Project architect Projektarchitekt Andrea Balducci Caste
Architects of record Lokale Architekten Planimetro
Client Bauherr CityLife SpA
Structural engineers Tragwerksplanung AKT; Redesco; Holzner & Bertagnolli Engineering; AIACE
MEP Haustechnik Max Fordham; Manens-TIFS; Deerns

Height Höhe 170 m
Storeys Geschosse 44
Gross floor area Bruttogeschossfläche 147 429 m²
Structure Konstruktion Reinforced concrete Stahlbeton
Completion Fertigstellung July Juli 2018
Main use Hauptnutzung Office Büros

Sustainability
Nachhaltigkeit

LEED Platinum Certified; ventilated double-skin façade with a series of ventilating registers in the glazing; sun-deflecting louvres; direct access to metro station
LEED-Platin-Zertifizierung; belüftete Doppelfassade mit zahlreichen Luftöffnungen in der Verglasung; Sonnenblenden; direkter Zugang zur Metrostation

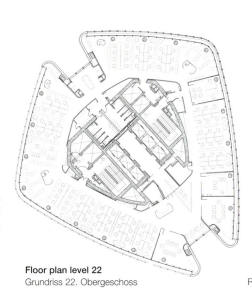

Floor plan level 22
Grundriss 22. Obergeschoss

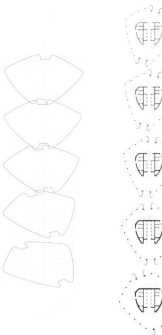

Rotation of floors
Rotation der Geschosse

The tower of the Generali insurance company – nicknamed 'Lo Storto' ('The Twisted One') – is located directly adjacent to two other recent high-rise buildings: Allianz Tower, nominated for the IHA 2016, and Libeskind Tower, still under construction. Together, they form the heart of the 366,000-square-metre CityLife master plan, which will occupy Milan's former trade fair grounds. At the centre of a public park which, in turn, is bordered by new residential developments, the three skyscrapers are grouped around a central square with a new underground metro station. Above the shopping centre housed in its plinth, the Generali Tower assumes the curving shape of the paths leading up to it, transforming it into a vertical vortex. Here, the building provides space for over 3,000 employees.

Following the anticipated completion of the master plan in 2020, CityLife, with its total of 1,000 residential apartments and 11,000 office spaces as well as 170,000 square metres of public space, will be Milan's largest urban development project of the last 120 years.

Der Turm des Versicherungsunternehmens Generali, im Volksmund auch „Lo Storto" (der Verdrehte) genannt, ist neben zwei weiteren Türmen (Allianz Tower, nominiert für den IHP 2016, sowie Libeskind Tower, noch im Bau) das Herzstück des 366 000 Quadratmeter umfassenden CityLife-Masterplans für das ehemalige Messegelände Mailands. Inmitten eines öffentlichen Parks, der wiederum von neuen Wohnquartieren gesäumt ist, gruppieren sich die Hochhäuser um einen zentralen Platz mit neuer, unterirdischer Metrostation. Über dem Einkaufszentrum im Sockel nimmt der Generali Tower den Schwung der ankommenden Fußwege auf und transformiert diese wirbelförmig in die Vertikale. Dort bietet das Gebäude Raum für mehr als 3000 Arbeitsplätze.

Nach der voraussichtlichen Fertigstellung des Masterplans im Jahr 2020 wird CityLife mit seinen insgesamt 1000 Wohnungen und 11 000 Büroarbeitsplätzen sowie 170 000 Quadratmetern öffentlichen Raums das größte Stadtentwicklungsprojekt der vergangenen 120 Jahre in Mailand sein.

The International Highrise Award Internationaler Hochhaus Preis **2018**

Nominated Project 2018
Nominiertes Projekt 2018

Zaha Hadid Architects
NANJING INTERNATIONAL CULTURAL CENTRE
Nanjing, China

Architects Architekten **Zaha Hadid Architects, London, UK** Großbritannien
Project architect Projektarchitekt **Shao-Wei Huang**
Architects of record Lokale Architekten **China Architecture Design Institute**
Client Bauherr **Hexi New Town Planning Bureau**
Structural engineers Tragwerksplanung **Buro Happold**
MEP Haustechnik **Buro Happold**

Height Höhe **315 m; 255 m**
Storeys Geschosse **68; 61**
Site area Grundstücksfläche **52 020 m²**
Gross floor area Bruttogeschossfläche **473 010 m²**
Structure Konstruktion **Steel** Stahl
Completion Fertigstellung **July** Juli **2018**

Main use Hauptnutzung **Mixed use comprising hotels, office and culture** Mischnutzung aus Hotels, Büros und Kultur

Sustainability
Nachhaltigkeit
Recycling facilities collect rainwater and filter it for outdoor irrigation; Combined Cooling Heating and Power (CCHP) system utilizes surplus heat steam from nearby power station for heating or cooling; double insulating glass curtain wall; energy monitoring for each management unit – for example, adjusting conditioned air volume according to number of users
Recycling-System sammelt und filtert Regenwasser für Bewässerung der Außenanlagen; Kraft-Wärme-Kälte-Koppelung nutzt Abwärme eines nahe gelegenen Kraftwerks zum Heizen und Kühlen; Vorhangfassade aus Zweifach-Isolierglas; Energiekontrolle jeder Versorgungseinheit steuert zum Beispiel Aktivität der Klimaanlage je nach Anzahl der Nutzer

Ground floor plan
Grundriss Erdgeschoss

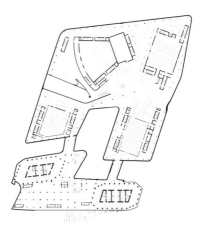

Floor plan 15 metres above ground
Grundriss in 15 Metern Höhe

Situated directly on the banks of the Yangtze River, this complex is part of the master plan for Nanjing's new central business district, 'Hexi New Town', which also includes the Financial City designed by gmp Architects (pp. 88–89). The five-storey pedestal – containing the conference centre that was opened early for the 2014 Youth Olympic Games – blends with the two towers to form a coherent sculpture with intriguing spatial sequences and interstices. At the transition between the towers and the pedestal, the glass façade crosses over fluidly into a lattice of diamond-shaped fibre-concrete modules. Their variously-sized openings create a moiré effect that emphasises the form's dynamic character.

In this way, the complex establishes a fluent relationship between the vertical modern buildings and the horizontal, rural character of the riverbank. To underline this, Zaha Hadid Architects initiated the construction of a footbridge linking the riverbank to the recreational area on the island opposite.

Direkt am Ufer des Jangtse gelegen ist der Komplex Teil des Masterplans für den neuen Central Business District (CBD) „Hexi New Town" von Nanjing, zu dem auch die Financial City aus dem Büro gmp (S. 88–89) gehört. Der 5-geschossige Sockelbau mit dem bereits vorab zur Jugendolympiade 2014 eröffneten Konferenzzentrum und die beiden Türme verschmelzen zu einer zusammenhängenden Skulptur mit spannenden Raumfolgen und Zwischenräumen. Am Übergang zwischen den Türmen und dem Sockel wechselt die Glasfassade fließend in ein Raster aus rhombischen Faserbetonmodulen. Deren verschieden große Öffnungen erzeugen einen Moiré-Effekt, der den dynamischen Charakter der Form betont.

So stellt der Komplex eine fließende Beziehung zwischen den vertikalen, modernen Gebäuden sowie dem horizontalen und noch ländlich geprägten Flussufer her. Zu diesem Zweck initiierten Zaha Hadid Architects auch eine neue Fußgängerbrücke, die das Ufer mit dem Naherholungsgebiet auf der gegenüberliegenden Flussinsel verbindet.

The International Highrise Award Internationaler Hochhaus Preis **2018** 135

Winners of the International Highrise Award
Preisträger Internationaler Hochhaus Preis
2004 – 2016

Award Winner Preisträger **2016**
VIA 57 WEST
New York NY, USA
Architects Architekten **BIG – Bjarke Ingels Group, Copenhagen** Kopenhagen, **Denmark** Dänemark / **New York**
Local architects Lokale Architekten **SLCE Architects, New York**
Client Bauherr **The Durst Organization, New York**

Award Winner Preisträger **2014**
BOSCO VERTICALE
Milan Mailand, **Italy** Italien
Architects Architekten **Boeri Studio, Milan** Mailand
Client Bauherr **Hines Italia SGR SpA, Milan** Mailand

Award Winner Preisträger **2012**
1 BLIGH STREET
Sydney, Australia Australien
Architects Architekten **ingenhoven architects, Dusseldorf** Düsseldorf, **Germany** Deutschland + **Architectus, Sydney**
Client Bauherr **DEXUS Property Group; DEXUS Wholesale Property Fund; Cbus Property, Sydney** (all alle)

Award Winner Preisträger **2010**
THE MET
Bangkok, Thailand
Architects Architekten **WOHA, Singapore** Singapur
Associated architects Assoziierte Architekten **Tandem Architects 2001 Co. Ltd, Bangkok**
Client Bauherr **Pebble Bay Thailand Co Ltd, Bangkok**

Award Winner Preisträger **2008**
HEARST HEADQUARTERS
New York NY, USA
Architects Architekten **Foster + Partners, London, UK** Großbritannien
Architects of record/shell and core Lokale Architekten/Rohbau **Adamson Associates, Toronto, Canada** Kanada
Client Bauherr **Hearst Corporation, New York**

Award Winner Preisträger **2006**
TORRE AGBAR
Barcelona, Spain Spanien
Architects Architekten **Ateliers Jean Nouvel, Paris, France** Frankreich
Client Bauherr **Layetana Developments, Barcelona**

Award Winner Preisträger **2004**
DE HOFTOREN
The Hague Den Haag, **Netherlands** Niederlande
Architects Architekten **Kohn Pedersen Fox Associates, London, UK** Großbritannien
Client Bauherr **ING Vastgoed, The Hague** Den Haag

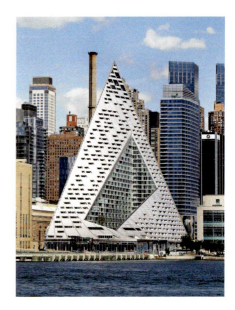

VIA 57 WEST
2016 New York NY, USA

BOSCO VERTICALE
2014 Milan Mailand, **Italy** Italien

1 BLIGH STREET
2012 Sydney, **Australia** Australien

THE MET
2010 Bangkok, Thailand

HEARST HEADQUARTERS
2008 New York NY, USA

TORRE AGBAR
2006 Barcelona, **Spain** Spanien

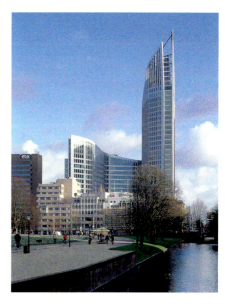

DE HOFTOREN
2004 **The Hague** Den Haag,
Netherlands Niederlande

List of Projects Projektliste
International Highrise Award Internationaler Hochhaus Preis
2004–2018

3D/International, Houston TX, USA
Carl B. Stokes Federal Courthouse, Cleveland OH, USA
Contribution Einreichung **2004**

ABB Architekten, Frankfurt, Germany
Bocom Financial Towers, Shanghai, China
Contribution Einreichung **2004**

Aedas, London, UK
Al Bahr Towers, Abu Dhabi, UAE
Nomination Nominierung **2014**

Aflalo & Gasperini Arquitectos, São Paulo, Brasil
Ventura Corporate Tower, Rio de Janeiro, Brasil
Nomination Nominierung **2012**

AL_A, London, UK
Central Embassy, Bangkok, Thailand
Nomination Nominierung **2018**

Amateur Architecture Studio, Hangzhou, China
Vertical Courtyard, Hangzhou, China
Nomination Nominierung **2008**

Andrea Maffei Architects, Milan, Italy
Allianz Tower, Milan, Italy
Nomination Nominierung **2016**

Arata Isozaki & Associates, Tokyo, Japan
Allianz Tower, Milan, Italy
Nomination Nominierung **2016**

Arc Studio Architecture + Urbanism, Singapore
Pinnacle@Duxton, Singapore
Finalist 2012

Architectus, Sydney, Australia
1 Bligh Street, Sydney, Australia
Prize Winner Preisträger **2012**

Arquitectonica International Corporation, Miami FL, USA
Landmark East, Hong Kong, China
Nomination Nominierung **2010**
Torun Tower, Istanbul, Turkey
Nomination Nominierung **2016**

Atelier Christian Portzamparc, Paris, France
One57, New York NY, USA
Nomination Nominierung **2014**

Ateliers Jean Nouvel, Paris, France
Torre Agbar, Barcelona, Spain
Prize Winner Preisträger **2006**
Doha Tower, Doha, Qatar
Nomination Nominierung **2014**
One Central Park, Sydney, Australia
Finalist 2014
Renaissance Barcelona Fira Hotel, Barcelona, Spain
Finalist 2014
Le Nouvel Ardmore, Singapore
Nomination Nominierung **2016**
Le Nouvel KLCC, Kuala Lumpur, Malaysia
Nomination Nominierung **2018**

Audrius Ambrasas Architects, Vilnius, Lithuania
Europa Tower, Vilnius, Lithuania
Contribution Einreichung **2004**

Atkins, Dubai, UAE
Bahrain World Trade Center, Manama, Bahrain
Nomination Nominierung **2008**

Baumschlager-Eberle, Lustenau, Austria
PopMoma, Beijing, China
Nomination Nominierung **2008**

BIG – Bjarke Ingels Group, Copenhagen, Denmark
VIA 57 West, New York NY, USA
Prize Winner Preisträger **2016**

Boeri Studio, Milan, Italy
Bosco Verticale, Milan, Italy
Prize Winner Preisträger **2014**

Building Design (Pvt) Ltd., Colombo, Sri Lanka
HNB Towers, Colombo, Sri Lanka
Contribution Einreichung **2004**

Büro Ole Scheeren, Beijing, China
CCTV Headquarters, Beijing, China
Nomination Nominierung **2014**
DUO, Singapore
Nomination Nominierung **2018**
MahaNakhon, Bangkok, Thailand
Finalist 2018

C. Y. Lee & Partners, Taipei, Taiwan
Taipei 101, Taipei, Taiwan
Nomination Nominierung **2006**

Carlos Zapata Studio, New York NY, USA
Bitexco Financial Tower, Ho Chi Minh City, Vietnam
Nomination Nominierung **2012**

CetraRuddy Architecture, New York NY, USA
One Madison Park, New York NY, USA
Nomination Nominierung **2012**

Cook + Fox Architects LLP, New York NY, USA
The Bank of America Tower, New York NY, USA
Nomination Nominierung **2010**

Coop Himmelb(l)au, Vienna, Austria
ECB – European Central Bank, Frankfurt, Germany
Nomination Nominierung **2016**

Cox Architecture, Sydney, Australia
Metro Residences Chatswood, Sydney, Australia
Nomination Nominierung **2016**

(desinged by) Erick van Egeraat, Rotterdam, Netherlands
Mercury City Tower, Moscow, Russia
Nomination Nominierung **2012**

Dam & Partners Architecten, Amsterdam, Netherlands
Maastoren, Rotterdam, Netherlands
Nomination Nominierung **2010**

David Chipperfield Architects, Berlin, Germany
Amorepacific Headquarters, Seoul, South Korea
Nomination Nominierung **2018**

Delugan Meissl Associated Architects, Vienna, Austria
Delugan Meissl Tower, Vienna, Austria
Finalist 2006

Dina Ammar – Avraham Curiel Architects, Haifa, Israel
The Sail Tower, Haifa, Israel
Contribution Einreichung **2004**

Dominique Perrault Architecture, Paris, France
ME Barcelona Hotel, Barcelona, Spain
Nomination Nominierung **2010**
Fukoku Tower, Osaka, Japan
Nomination Nominierung **2012**
DC Tower I, Vienna, Austria
Nomination Nominierung **2014**

Donovan Hill, Brisbane, Australia
Santos Place, Brisbane, Australia
Nomination Nominierung **2010**

Ellerbe Becket, Minneapolis MN, USA
Kingdom Centre, Riyadh, Saudi Arabia
Contribution Einreichung **2004**

EMBA_Estudi Massip-Bosch Arquitectes, Barcelona, Spain
Torre Telefónica Tower, Barcelona, Spain
Nomination Nominierung **2012**

Fender Katsalidis Architects, Melbourne, Australia
Eureka Tower, Melbourne, Australia
Nomination Nominierung **2008**

Foster + Partners, London, UK
30 St Mary Axe, London, UK
Finalist 2004
Deutsche Bank Place, Sydney, Australia
Nomination Nominierung **2006**
Hearst Headquarters, New York NY, USA
Prize Winner Preisträger **2008**
Regent Place, Sydney, Australia
Nomination Nominierung **2008**
The Willis Building, London, UK
Nomination Nominierung **2008**
Jameson House, Vancouver, Canada
Nomination Nominierung **2012**
The Index, Dubai, UAE
Nomination Nominierung **2012**

The Troika, Kuala Lumpur, Malaysia
Finalist 2012
The Bow, Calgary, Canada
Nomination Nominierung 2014
Burj Mohammed Bin Rashid + World Trade Center, Abu Dhabi, UAE
Nomination Nominierung 2016
South Beach, Singapore
Nomination Nominierung 2016
UN Plaza, New York NY, USA
Nomination Nominierung 2016
The Bund Finance Center, Shanghai, China
Nomination Nominierung 2018

Francis-Jones Morehen Thorp, Sydney, Australia
EY Centre, Sydney, Australia
Nomination Nominierung 2018

Frank Williams & Associates, New York NY, USA
Mercury City Tower, Moscow, Russia
Nomination Nominierung 2014

Gatermann + Schossig, Cologne, Germany
KölnTriangle, Cologne, Germany
Nomination Nominierung 2006

Gehry Partners LLP, Los Angeles CA, USA
Eight Spruce Street, New York NY, USA
Finalist 2012

Gensler, San Francisco CA, USA
Shanghai Tower, Shanghai, China
Nomination Nominierung 2016

Gerber Architekten, Dortmund, Germany
RWE Tower, Dortmund, Germany
Nomination Nominierung 2006

Gigon/Guyer Architekten, Zurich, Switzerland
Prime Tower, Zurich, Switzerland
Nomination Nominierung 2012

GKK+ Architekten, Berlin, Germany
Hauptverwaltung Süddeutscher Verlag, Munich, Germany
Nomination Nominierung 2010

gmp Architekten von Gerkan, Marg und Partner, Hamburg, Germany
Guangzhou Development Central Building, Guangzhou, China
Nomination Nominierung 2006
Wanda Plaza, Beijing, China
Nomination Nominierung 2008
Neue Deutsche Bank Towers (revitalisation), Frankfurt, Germany
Special Rec. Bes. Anerkennung 2012
Bund SOHO, Shanghai, China
Nomination Nominierung 2016
Greenland Central Plaza, Zhengzhou, China
Nomination Nominierung 2018
Nanjing Financial City, Nanjing, China
Nomination Nominierung 2018

Goettsch Partners, Chicago IL, USA
150 North Riverside, Chicago IL, USA
Nomination Nominierung 2018

Gruber + Kleine-Kraneburg Architekten, Frankfurt, Germany
TaunusTurm, Frankfurt, Germany
Nomination Nominierung 2014

Harry Gugger Studio, Basel, Switzerland
The Exchange, Vancouver, Canada
Nomination Nominierung 2018

Harry Seidler and Associates, Sydney, Australia
The Cove, Sydney, Australia
Finalist 2004
Riparian Plaza, Brisbane, Australia
Nomination Nominierung 2006
Meriton Tower, Sydney, Australia
Nomination Nominierung 2008

Heatherwick Studio, London, UK
The Bund Finance Center, Shanghai, China
Nomination Nominierung 2018

Heller Manus Architects, San Francisco CA, USA
181 Fremont, San Francisco CA, USA
Nomination Nominierung 2018

Herzog & de Meuron, Basel, Switzerland
56 Leonard Street, New York NY, USA
Nomination Nominierung 2018
Beirut Terraces, Beirut, Lebanon
Finalist 2018

Ian Moore Architects, Manchester, UK
Air Apartments, Broadbeach/Queensland, Australia
Nomination Nominierung 2008

Ian Simpson Architects, Manchester, UK
Beetham Hilton Tower, Manchester, UK
Nomination Nominierung 2008
Holloway Circus, Birmingham, UK
Nomination Nominierung 2008

ingenhoven architects, Dusseldorf, Germany
Uptown München, Munich, Germany
Nomination Nominierung 2006
Breezé Tower, Osaka, Japan
Nomination Nominierung 2010
1 Bligh Street, Sydney, Australia
Prize Winner Preisträger 2012
Marina One, Singapore
Nomination Nominierung 2018

JAHN, Chicago IL, USA
Cosmopolitan Twarda 2/4, Warsaw, Poland
Nomination Nominierung 2016
50 West, New York NY, USA
Nomination Nominierung 2018

John Lee/Michael Timchula Architects, New York NY, USA
Shenzhen World Trade Center, Shenzhen, China
Contribution Einreichung 2004

Johnson Fain, Los Angeles CA, USA
Constellation Palace, Los Angeles CA, USA
Contribution Einreichung 2004

J.S.K. International Architekten und Ingenieure, Frankfurt, Germany
Tornado Tower, Doha, Qatar
Nomination Nominierung 2010

Kallmann Mckinnell & Wood Architects, Boston MA, USA
Carl B. Stokes Federal Courthouse, Cleveland OH, USA
Contribution Einreichung 2004

KCAP Architects & Planners, Rotterdam, Netherlands
The Red Apple, Rotterdam, Netherlands
Nomination Nominierung 2010

Kohn Pedersen Fox Associates PC, New York NY, USA
De Hoftoren, The Hague, Netherlands
Prize Winner Preisträger 2004
Roppongi Hills Mori Tower, Tokyo, Japan
Contribution Einreichung 2004
Adia Headquarters, Abu Dhabi, UAE
Nomination Nominierung 2008
International Commerce Center, Hong Kong, China
Nomination Nominierung 2010
Shanghai World Financial Center, Shanghai, China
Finalist 2010
Ventura Corporate Tower, Rio de Janeiro, Brasil
Nomination Nominierung 2012
Lotte World Tower, Seoul, South Korea
Nomination Nominierung 2018
Ping An Finance Centre, Shenzhen, China
Nomination Nominierung 2018

KSP Jürgen Engel Architekten, Frankfurt, Germany
WestendDuo, Frankfurt, Germany
Special Rec. Bes. Anerkennung 2008
Palais Quartier Office Tower, Frankfurt, Germany
Nomination Nominierung 2010

Kuwabara Payne McKenna Blumberg Architects, Toronto, Canada
Manitoba Hydro Place, Winnipeg, Canada
Nomination Nominierung 2010

L. Benjamin Romano, Mexico City, Mexico
Torre Reforma, Mexico City, Mexico
Prize Winner Preisträger 2018

Legorreta, Mexico City, Mexico
Torre BBVA Bancomer, Mexico City, Mexico
Nomination Nominierung 2016

Louis Karlsberger & Associates, Columbus OH, USA
Carl B. Stokes Federal Courthouse, Cleveland OH, USA
Contribution Einreichung 2004

M. M. Posokhin, Moscow, Russia
Mercury City Tower, Moscow, Russia
Nomination Nominierung **2012**

MAD Architects, Beijing, China
Absolute World Towers, Mississauga, Canada
Finalist 2012
Sheraton Huzhou Hot Spring Resort, Huzhou, China
Nomination Nominierung **2014**
Fake Hills (Part 1), Beihai, China
Nomination Nominierung **2016**
Chaoyang Park Plaza, Beijing, China
Finalist 2018

Maki & Associates, Tokyo, Japan
4 World Trade Center, New York NY, USA
Finalist 2016

Mario Bellini Architects, Milan, Italy
Neue Deutsche Bank Towers, Frankfurt, Germany
Special Rec. Bes. Anerkennung **2012**

Mario Botta Architetto, Mendrisio, Switzerland
Kyobo Gangnam Tower, Seoul, South Korea
Finalist 2004

Mass Studies, Seoul, South Korea
Missing Matrix Building, Seoul, South Korea
Finalist 2008
S-trenue: Bundle Matrix, Seoul, South Korea
Nomination Nominierung **2010**

Mecanoo Architecten, Rotterdam, Netherlands
Montevideo, Rotterdam, Netherlands
Finalist 2006

Meixner Schlüter Wendt Architekten, Frankfurt, Germany
Neuer Henninger Turm, Frankfurt, Germany
Nomination Nominierung **2018**

Mitsubishi Jisho Sekkei Inc., Tokyo, Japan
Breezé Tower, Osaka, Japan
Nomination Nominierung **2010**

Morger & Degelo, Marques, Basel, Switzerland
Basler Messeturm, Basel, Switzerland
Contribution Einreichung **2004**

Murphy/Jahn Architects, Chicago IL, USA
Post Tower, Bonn, Germany
Contribution Einreichung **2004**
Highlight Towers, Munich, Germany
Nomination Nominierung **2006**
Veer Towers, Las Vegas NV, USA
Nomination Nominierung **2012**

MVSA – Meyer en Van Schooten Architecten, Amsterdam, Netherlands
New Babylon, The Hague, Netherlands
Nomination Nominierung **2012**

NBBJ, Seattle WA, USA
Tencent Seafront Headquarters, Shenzhen, China
Nomination Nominierung **2018**

Novotny Mähner Assoziierte, Offenbach, Germany
Gallileo, Frankfurt, Germany
Contribution Einreichung **2004**

nps tchoban voss, Hamburg, Germany
Federation Towers, Moscow, Russia
Nomination Nominierung **2016**

OMA Office for Metropolitan Architecture, Rotterdam/Beijing, Netherlands/China
TVCC – Television Cultural Center, Beijing, China
Finalist 2008
Shenzhen Stock Exchange, Shenzhen, China
Nomination Nominierung **2010**
CCTV Headquarters, Beijing, China
Nomination Nominierung **2014**
De Rotterdam, Rotterdam, Netherlands
Finalist 2014
MahaNakhon, Bangkok, Thailand
Finalist 2018

Paul Davis & Partners, London, UK
Grosvenor Place, Hong Kong, China
Contribution Einreichung **2004**

Pei Cobb Freed & Partners Architects LLP, New York NY, USA
Torre Espacio, Madrid, Spain
Nomination Nominierung **2008**

Pelli Clarke Pelli Architects, New Haven CT, USA
Two International Finance Center, Hong Kong, China
Nomination Nominierung **2006**
Torre Costanera, Santiago, Chile
Nomination Nominierung **2014**
Salesforce Tower, San Francisco CA, USA
Nomination Nominierung **2018**

Perkins + Will, Chicago IL, USA
235 West Van Buren, Chicago IL, USA
Nomination Nominierung **2010**

Prof. Christoph Mäckler Architekten, Frankfurt, Germany
OpernTurm, Frankfurt, Germany
Nomination Nominierung **2010**
Zoofenster – Waldorf Astoria Berlin, Berlin, Germany
Nomination Nominierung **2014**

querkraft architekten, Vienna, Austria
Citygate Tower & Leopold Tower, Vienna, Austria
Nomination Nominierung **2016**

R&AS Rubio & Álvarez-Sala, Madrid, Spain
Torre SyV, Madrid, Spain
Nomination Nominierung **2008**

Rafael de La-Hoz Arquitectos, Madrid, Spain
Las Torres de Hércules, Los Barrios, Spain
Nomination Nominierung **2010**

Rafael Viñoly Architects, New York NY, USA
432 Park Avenue, New York NY, USA
Finalist 2016

Rapp & Rapp, Amsterdam, Netherlands
De Kroon, The Hague, Netherlands
Nomination Nominierung **2014**

Reiser + Umemoto, RUR Architecture PC, New York NY, USA
O-14, Dubai, UAE
Nomination Nominierung **2010**

Renzo Piano Building Workshop, Genoa, Italy
New York Times Building, New York NY, USA
Finalist 2008
The Shard London Bridge Tower, London, UK
Nomination Nominierung **2014**
Tribunal de Paris, Paris, France
Nomination Nominierung **2018**

Research Architecture Design Ltd., Hong Kong, China
SK Telecom Headquarters, Seoul, South Korea
Nomination Nominierung **2006**

Richard Meier & Partners Architects, New York NY, USA
Rothschild Tower, Tel Aviv, Israel
Nomination Nominierung **2016**

Riken Yamamoto & Field Shop, Yokohama, Japan
Jian Wai Soho, Beijing, China
Finalist 2006

Robert A. M. Stern Architects LLP, New York NY, USA
Comcast Center, Philadelphia PA, USA
Nomination Nominierung **2010**

Roberto Perez-Guerras Architects, Madrid, Spain
Neguri Gane, Benidorm, Spain
Contribution Einreichung **2004**

Rocco Design Architects Ltd., Hong Kong, China
One Beijing Road, Hong Kong, China
Contribution Einreichung **2004**

Richard Rogers Partnership, London, UK
Hesperia Hotel and Conference Center, L'Hospitalet/Barcelona, Spain
Nomination Nominierung **2008**

Rogers Stirk Harbour & Partners, London, UK
8 Chifley Square, Sydney, Australia
Nomination Nominierung **2014**
The Leadenhall, London, UK
Nomination Nominierung **2014**
Torre BBVA Bancomer, Mexico City, Mexico
Nomination Nominierung **2016**

SAA Schweger Associated Architects, Hamburg, Germany
Federation Towers, Moscow, Russia
Nomination Nominierung 2016

Safdie Architects, Somerville MA, USA
SkyHabitat, Singapore
Finalist 2016

Santiago Calatrava LLC, Zurich, Switzerland
HSB Turning Torso, Malmö, Sweden
Finalist 2006

SCDA Architects, Singapore
SkyTerrace @ Dawson, Singapore
Nomination Nominierung 2016
Echelon, Singapore
Nomination Nominierung 2018

schneider + schumacher, Frankfurt, Germany
Westhafen Tower, Frankfurt, Germany
Contribution Einreichung 2004
Silver Tower (revitalisiation), Frankfurt, Germany
Nomination Nominierung 2010

SHoP Architects, New York NY, USA
461 Dean Street, New York NY, USA
Nomination Nominierung 2018
American Copper Buildings, New York NY, USA
Nomination Nominierung 2018

SimpsonHaugh, London, UK
Dollar Bay, London, UK
Nomination Nominierung 2018

Skidmore, Owings & Merrill LLP, Chicago IL, USA
Tower Palace III, Seoul, South Korea
Nomination Nominierung 2006
7 World Trade Center, New York NY, USA
Nomination Nominierung 2008
Burj Khalifa, Dubai, UAE
Special Rec. Bes. Anerkennung 2010
The Broadgate Tower, London, UK
Nomination Nominierung 2010
Trump International Hotel & Tower, Chicago IL, USA
Nomination Nominierung 2010
Tianjin Global Financial Center, Tianjin, China
Nomination Nominierung 2012
Cayan Tower, Dubai, UAE
Nomination Nominierung 2014
Pearl River Tower, Guangzhou, China
Nomination Nominierung 2014
1 World Trade Center, New York NY, USA
Nomination Nominierung 2016
Baccarat Hotel & Residences, New York NY, USA
Nomination Nominierung 2016
Jiangxi Nanchang Greenland Central Plaza, Nanchang, China
Nomination Nominierung 2016
Poly International Plaza, Beijing, China
Nomination Nominierung 2018
The Lexicon, London, UK
Nomination Nominierung 2018

Somdoon Architects, Bangkok, Thailand
Ideo Morph 38, Bangkok, Thailand
Nomination Nominierung 2014

Squire & Partners, London, UK
The Lexicon, London, UK
Nomination Nominierung 2018

Steidle + Partner, Munich, Germany
Chaowei Men, Beijing, China
Nomination Nominierung 2008

Steven Holl Architects, New York NY, USA
Sliced Porosity Block – Raffles City Chengdu, Chengdu, China
Finalist 2014

Studio Daniel Libeskind, New York NY, USA
Reflections at Keppel Bay, Singapore
Nomination Nominierung 2012

Studio Gang Architects Ltd., Chicago IL, USA
Aqua Tower, Chicago IL, USA
Finalist 2010

T. R. Hamzah & Yeang Sdn. Bhd., Ampang Selanger, Malaysia
Singapore National Library, Singapore
Nomination Nominierung 2006

Tabanlioglu Architects, Istanbul, Turkey
Sapphire, Istanbul, Turkey
Nomination Nominierung 2012

Tago Architects, Istanbul, Turkey
Dumankaya Ikon, Istanbul, Turkey
Nomination Nominierung 2014

Takenaka Corporation, Osaka, Japan
Abeno Harukas, Osaka, Japan
Nomination Nominierung 2016

Tange Associates, Tokyo, Japan
Mode Gakuen Cocoon Tower, Tokyo, Japan
Finalist 2010
One Raffles Place Tower 2, Singapore
Nomination Nominierung 2012

Tectum Architects, Riga, Latvia
Hansabanka Central Office, Riga, Latvia
Nomination Nominierung 2006

TEN Arquitectos, New York NY, USA
Mercedes House, New York NY, USA
Nomination Nominierung 2014

TFP Farrells, London, UK
KK 100, Shenzhen, China
Nomination Nominierung 2012

Toyo Ito & Associates, Tokyo, Japan
CapitaGreen, Singapore
Nomination Nominierung 2016

UNStudio, Amsterdam, Netherlands
Ardmore Residence, Singapore
Nomination Nominierung 2014
Raffles City, Hangzhou, China
Nomination Nominierung 2018
The Scotts Tower, Singapore
Nomination Nominierung 2018

Valode & Pistre Architects, Paris, France
T1 Tower, Paris, France
Nomination Nominierung 2010

Wilkinson Eyre Architects, London, UK
Guangzhou International Finance Center, Guangzhou, China
Nomination Nominierung 2012

Wingårdh Arkitektenkontor AB, Gothenburg, Sweden
Victoria Tower, Stockholm, Sweden
Nomination Nominierung 2012

WOHA, Singapore
Newton Suites, Singapore
Finalist 2008
The Met, Bangkok, Thailand
Prize Winner Preisträger 2010
SkyVille @ Dawson, Singapore
Finalist 2016
Huaku Sky Garden, Taipei, Taiwan
Nomination Nominierung 2018
Oasia Hotel Downtown, Singapore
Finalist 2018

Zaha Hadid Architects, London, UK
CMA CGM Head Office Tower, Marseille, France
Nomination Nominierung 2012
D'Leedon, Singapore
Nomination Nominierung 2016
Wangjing SOHO, Beijing, China
Nomination Nominierung 2016
Generali Tower, Milan, Italy
Nomination Nominierung 2018
Nanjing International Cultural Centre, Nanjing, China
Nomination Nominierung 2018

Imprint: Project Coordination
Impressum Projektkoordination

Stadt Frankfurt am Main

DAM Deutsches Architekturmuseum:
Peter Cachola Schmal, Director Direktor
Peter Körner, Coordination Koordination
Maximilian Liesner, Coordination Koordination
Stefanie Lampe, Public Relations Öffentlichkeitsarbeit
Inka Plechaty, Jacqueline Brauer, Administration Verwaltung

Department for Culture and Science:
Dezernat Kultur und Wissenschaft:
Jana Kremin, Press Officer and Head of Public Relations Pressesprecherin und Leiterin der Öffentlichkeitsarbeit

DekaBank

Silke Schuster-Müller, Head of Corporate Social Responsibility Leiterin Gesellschaftliches Engagement
Valery Trosdorf, Corporate Social Responsibility Gesellschaftliches Engagement
Sonja Walentin, Corporate Social Responsibility Gesellschaftliches Engagement
Björn Korschinowski, Head of Corporate Communications Leiter Unternehmenskommunikation
Dr. Daniela Gniss, Press Officer Referentin Unternehmenskommunikation

Event Organisation Veranstaltungsorganisation
Jazzunique GmbH, Frankfurt am Main
Steffen Weber, Cansu Celik

Media partner Medienpartner:

Meeting of the Jury
Jurysitzung
DekaBank (Trianon High-rise Hochhaus), Frankfurt am Main

Members of the Jury Mitglieder der Jury 2018:
Kai-Uwe Bergmann (Jury chairman Juryvorsitzender), Architect Architekt / Partner, BIG – Bjarke Ingels Group, New York City / Copenhagen Kopenhagen
Sean Anderson, Associate Curator for Architecture and Design Kurator für Architektur und Design, Museum of Modern Art MoMA, New York City
Dr. Ina Hartwig, Deputy Mayor in charge of Culture Kulturdezernentin, Frankfurt am Main
Jette Cathrin Hopp, Project Director Projektleiterin / Senior Architect Leitende Architektin, Snøhetta, Oslo
Peter Cachola Schmal, Director Direktor Deutsches Architekturmuseum DAM, Frankfurt am Main
Thomas Schmengler, Managing Director Geschäftsführer, Deka Immobilien GmbH, Frankfurt am Main
Knut Stockhusen, Structural engineer Tragwerksplaner / Partner, schlaich bergermann partner, Stuttgart

Substitutional Members Stellvertretende Jurymitglieder
Prof. Ulrike Lauber, Architect Architektin / Principal Geschäftsführerin, lauber zottmann blank architekten, Munich München
Horst R. Muth, Head of Real Estate Management Leiter Projektmanagement Immobilien, Deka Immobilien GmbH, Frankfurt am Main

Imprint: Catalogue
Impressum Katalog

This catalogue has been published in conjunction with the exhibition "Best Highrises 2018/19", organized by the Deutsches Architekturmuseum, Department of Culture and Science, Frankfurt am Main, Germany, taking place from 03 November 2018 till 03 March 2019 at Deutsches Architekturmuseum, Frankfurt am Main.
Dieser Katalog erscheint anlässlich der Ausstellung „Best Highrises 2018/19" des Deutschen Architekturmuseums, Dezernat Kultur und Wissenschaft, Stadt Frankfurt am Main vom 03. November 2018 bis zum 03. März 2019 im Deutschen Architekturmuseum, Frankfurt am Main.

© Prestel Verlag, Munich · London · New York 2018

The copyright on the texts is held by the respective author.
Das Copyright für die Texte liegt bei den Autoren.
The copyright on the pictures is held by the respective photographer / holder of the picture rights.
Das Copyright für die Abbildungen liegt bei den Fotografen / Inhabern der Bildrechte.
The copyright on the layout is held by the graphic designers.
Das Copyright für die Gestaltung liegt bei den Grafikdesignern.

Prestel Verlag, Munich
A member of Verlagsgruppe Random House GmbH
Neumarkter Straße 28
81673 Munich
www.prestel.de

Prestel Publishing Ltd.
14-17 Wells Street
London W1T 3PD

Prestel Publishing
900 Broadway, Suite 603
New York, NY 10003
www.prestel.com

A CIP catalogue record for this book is available from the British Library.

In respect to links in the book, Verlagsgruppe Random House expressly notes that no illegal content was discernible on the linked sites at the time the links were created. The Publisher has no influence at all over the current and future design, content or authorship of the linked sites. For this reason Verlagsgruppe Random House expressly disassociates itself from all content on linked sites that has been altered since the link was created and assumes no liability for such content.
Der Verlag weist ausdrücklich darauf hin, dass im Text enthaltene externe Links vom Verlag nur bis zum Zeitpunkt der Buchveröffentlichung eingesehen werden konnten. Auf spätere Veränderungen hat der Verlag keinerlei Einfluss. Eine Haftung des Verlags ist daher ausgeschlossen.

All rights reserved Alle Rechte vorbehalten

Editors Herausgeber
Peter Körner, Maximilian Liesner, Peter Cachola Schmal

Editing Redaktion
Peter Körner, Maximilian Liesner, Stefanie Lampe

Copyediting (German) Lektorat (deutsch)
Dr. Willfried Baatz

Copyediting (English) Lektorat (englisch)
David Shallis

Translations German – English Übersetzungen Deutsch – Englisch
Mary Dobrian
Jeremy Gaines, Frankfurt am Main

Translations English – German Übersetzungen Englisch – Deutsch
Brigitte Rüßmann & Wolfgang Beuchelt – Scriptorium, Cologne Köln

Proofreading Endkorrektorat
Ute Thomsen

Graphic Design Gestaltung
Studio Joachim Mildner, Cologne Köln / Zurich Zürich

Cover Umschlagfoto
Moritz Bernoully, Frankfurt am Main / Mexico City Mexiko-Stadt

Coordination publishing house Koordination im Verlag
Laura Ilse

Production Herstellung
Corinna Pickart

Lithography Lithografie
Lars Scharrenbroich, Cologne Köln

Printing and binding Druck und Bindung
aprinta druck GmbH, Wemding

Paper Papier
Condat matt Périgord

Verlagsgruppe Random House FSC® N001967

ISBN 978-3-7913-5831-4

Imprint: Exhibition
Impressum Ausstellung

Director Direktor DAM
Peter Cachola Schmal

Deputy Director Stellvertretende Direktorin
Andrea Jürges

Curators Kuratoren
Peter Körner, Maximilian Liesner

Exhibition design Ausstellungsgestaltung
Deserve Gbr Raum und Medien Design, Wiesbaden / Berlin, Mario Lorenz

Exhibition production Ausstellungsproduktion
inditec GmbH, Bad Camberg
Schreinerei Oliver Taschke, Offenbach

Director exhibit setup Leitung Ausstellungsaufbau
Christian Walter

Exhibit setup Ausstellungsaufbau
Ömer Simsek, Gerhard Winkler

Registrar Registrar
Wolfgang Welker

Models Modelle
Büro Ole Scheeren, Bangkok
Herzog & de Meuron, Basel
MAD Architects, Beijing Peking
L. Benjamín Romano, Mexico-City Mexiko-Stadt
WOHA, Singapore Singapur

Model restoration Modellrestaurierung
Christian Walter

Public Relations Öffentlichkeitsarbeit
Stefanie Lampe, Brita Köhler, Rebekka Rass

Education Architekturvermittlung
Christina Budde

Guided tours Führungen
Yorck Förster

Administrative staff Sekretariat und Verwaltung
Inka Plechaty, Jacqueline Brauer

Museum technician Haustechnik
Joachim Müller-Rahn

Interns Praktikantinnen
Hanna Thiel, Kira Zisch

Graphic design printmedia Gestaltung Printmedien
Gardeners, Frankfurt am Main

Graphic design Gestaltung
The International Highrise Award
Internationaler Hochhaus Preis
Studio Joachim Mildner, Cologne Köln / Zurich Zürich

For its generous funding, DAM wishes to thank its partner
Danksagung für großzügige finanzielle Unterstützung
DekaBank
Sponsor of the International Highrise Award and the exhibition
Stifter des Internationalen Hochhaus Preises und der Ausstellung

With special acknowledgements to
Mit besonderem Dank an
Emma Aulanko, Grace Birrell, Horst Brandenburg, Charlotte Breuillé, Margherita Cardoso, Kiran Chapman, Andrea Chin, Alessandra Ciampi, Taylor Coe, Mary Dymond, Davide Giardano, Katy Harris, Edward Haynes, Jessica Heller, Chris Hepner, Haron Kababie, Serena Khor, Maike Klothen, Melissa Kraby, Michael Kuhn, Anna Kwon, Sakis Kyratzis, Matt Larson, Anke Lawrence, Emilie Lemons, Lilian Levy Salame, Rachel Lexier-Nagle, Julie Manière, Maria Marques, Hannah Martin-Merchant, Vanessa Martins, Véronique Moine, Furio Montoli, Judith Opferkuch, Kevin Ou, Tae-Ry Park, Stephanie Pelzer, Niki Pliakogianni, Rachel Prance, Katharina Ricklefs, Ariel Rosenstock, Maria Roßmann, Danijela Simovic, Binky Spolarich, Claudia Tiesler, Julia van Ekeris, Nathalie Weiss, Janet Yoder

Picture Credits Abbildungsnachweise

Cover Umschlag
Torre Reforma, Mexico City Mexiko-Stadt
Photo Foto Moritz Bernoully, Frankfurt am Main / Mexico City Mexiko-Stadt

Foreword Vorwort
4–5 Kirsten Bucher; 7 left links Wolfgang Günzel, right rechts Kirsten Bucher

Prize Winner Preisträger 2018
8 Alfonso Merchand; 11–13 Iwan Baan; 14 LBR&A Arquitectos; 15 Iwan Baan; 16 Santiago Arau; 17 top oben Moritz Bernoully, bottom unten Santiago Arau; 18 LBR&A Arquitectos; 19–21 Moritz Bernoully; 22 top oben Alfonso Merchand, bottom left unten links Moritz Bernoully, bottom right unten rechts Iwan Baan; 23 Moritz Bernoully; 25 top left oben links Alfonso Merchand, top right oben rechts LBR&A Arquitectos, bottom both unten beide Moritz Bernoully; 26 top oben Moritz Bernoully, bottom both unten beide Iwan Baan; 28 Santiago Arau; 29 Moritz Bernoully; 30 photos Fotos Moritz Bernoully, plans Pläne LBR&A Arquitectos; 31 Iwan Baan; 33 Moritz Bernoully; 34 Iwan Baan; 35 Moritz Bernoully; 36–37 Santiago Arau; 39 top oben Moritz Bernoully, bottom unten Santiago Arau; 40 Moritz Bernoully; 41 top both oben beide Moritz Bernoully, bottom unten Alfonso Merchand; 42 bottom right unten rechts Iwan Baan, all others alle anderen Moritz Bernoully; 44 Foster + Partners; 45 Alfonso Merchand; 47 Moritz Bernoully

Finalists Finalisten 2018
50 Büro Ole Scheeren / HLS; 51 Alexander Roan; 52 top oben Hufton + Crow, bottom both unten beide Büro Ole Scheeren / HLS; 53 Büro Ole Scheeren / HLS; 54 top right oben rechts Büro Ole Scheeren / HLS, bottom left unten links Iwan Baan, all others alle anderen Hufton + Crow; 56 Herzog & de Meuron; 57 Iwan Baan; 58 top oben Benchmark Development / Mohammad Al Kurdi, centre Mitte Bahaa Ghoussainy, bottom unten Iwan Baan; 59 Bahaa Ghoussainy; 60 Herzog & de Meuron; 61 left links Herzog & de Meuron, right rechts Bahaa Ghoussainy; 62 MAD Architects; 63 Hufton + Crow; 64 top oben Huang Mingxian, centre Mitte Iwan Baan, bottom all unten alle Hufton + Crow; 66 MAD Architects; 67 Hufton + Crow; 68 WOHA; 69 K. Kopter; 70 top left oben links Patrick Bingham-Hall, centre right Mitte rechts Darren Soh, all others alle anderen K. Kopter; 72 WOHA; 73 Patrick Bingham-Hall

Projects Nominated Nominierte Projekte 2018
74 AL_A; 75 top oben Edward Barnieh, bottom left unten links Hufton + Crow, bottom right unten rechts AL_A; 76 Ateliers Jean Nouvel; 77 Roland Halbe; 78 Büro Ole Scheeren; 79 Iwan Baan; 80 David Chipperfield Architects; 81 Noshe; 82 Foster + Partners and Heatherwick Studio; 83 bottom right unten rechts Foster + Partners, all others alle anderen Laurian Ghinitoiu; 84 Francis-Jones Morehen Thorp; 85 left links Brett Boardman, right both rechts beide Rodrigo Vargas; 86 gmp Architekten von Gerkan, Marg und Partner; 87 Zeng Jianghe; 88 gmp Architekten von Gerkan, Marg und Partner; 89 HG Esch; 90 Goettsch Partners; 91 bottom centre unten Mitte James Florio, all others alle anderen Tom Rossiter; 92 Harry Gugger Studio; 93 top both oben beide Courtesy of Credit Suisse, bottom left unten links Martin Tessler; 94 Heller Manus Architects; 95 top both oben beide Heller Manus Architects, bottom left unten links Florent Lamoureux; 96 Herzog & de Meuron; 97 bottom right unten rechts Hufton + Crow, all others alle anderen Iwan Baan; 98 ingenhoven architects; 99 HG Esch; 100 JAHN; 101 top left oben links Qualls Benson, top right oben rechts Rainer Viertlböck, bottom unten Tom Rossiter; 102 Kohn Pedersen Fox Associates; 103 Tim Griffith; 104 Kohn Pedersen Fox Associates; 105 Tim Griffith; 106 Meixner Schlüter Wendt Architekten; 107 Norbert Miguletz; 108 NBBJ; 109 Tim Griffith; 110 Pelli Clarke Pelli Architects; 111 bottom right unten rechts Vittoria Zupicich; all others alle anderen Tim Griffith; 112 Renzo Piano Building Workshop; 113 top left oben links Sergio Grazia, top right oben rechts Ph. Guignard / air-images.net, bottom left unten links Michel Denancé, bottom right unten rechts Renzo Piano Building Workshop; 114 SCDA Architects; 115 bottom right unten rechts SCDA Architects, all others alle anderen Aaron Pocock; 116 SHoP Architects; 117 top right oben rechts Max Touhey, all others alle anderen SHoP Architects; 118 SHoP Architects; 119 top oben SHoP Architects, bottom left unten links Max Touhey, bottom centre unten Mitte Field Condition, bottom right unten rechts Pavel Bendov; 120 SimpsonHaugh; 121 bottom left unten links Ben Anders, all others alle anderen Hufton + Crow; 122 Skidmore, Owings & Merrill LLP; 123 Bruce Damonte; 124 Skidmore, Owings & Merrill LLP; 125 top oben Paul Raftery, bottom left unten links Ben Veasey, bottom right unten rechts Skidmore, Owings & Merrill LLP; 126 UNStudio; 127 top both oben beide Hufton + Crow, bottom both unten beide Seth Powers; 128 UNStudio; 129 bottom left unten links Edmon Leong, all others alle anderen Darren Soh; 130 WOHA; 131 top left oben links Flyht Studio, all others alle anderen Patrick Bingham-Hall; 132 Zaha Hadid Architects; 133 Hufton + Crow; 134 Zaha Hadid Architects; 135 Hufton + Crow

Winners of the International Highrise Award Preisträger Internationaler Hochhaus Preis 2004–2016
136 Kirsten Bucher; 137 top centre oben Mitte HG Esch, bottom left unten links Chuck Choi, bottom centre unten Mitte Thomas Spier, bottom right unten rechts Y. Chea Park, all others alle anderen Kirsten Bucher